"We seem to accumulate [___] like so many sticky notes attached all over him, until we can no longer see him beneath our labels. We also tend to be unaware that we've done this until someone like Matt comes along and helps us to see ourselves and Jesus more clearly. Matt has paired his clever writing style—which I've long admired—with his years of real-world theological reflection and self-examination to offer us an entertaining read with piercing theological insight. Enjoy."

> **Mike Wilkerson,** President of Redemption Groups Network; author of *Redemption: Freed by Jesus from the Idols We Worship and the Wounds We Carry*

"I don't know when I've laughed so hard, thought so deeply, and repented so much while reading a book. *Getting Jesus Wrong* is an amazing life-altering book. When I said "life-altering" everything you thought I said is wrong. Read it, find out why and give this book to everyone you know."

> **Steve Brown,** Key Life radio broadcaster; author of *Hidden Agendas* and *How to Talk So People Will Listen*

"The usual 'answer' to disillusionment with evangelical and Pentecostal church life is growing resentment, actual personal despair, and almost inevitable distancing. But it doesn't have to be this way! Matt Johnson's book helps disillusioned Christians find the Real Thing underneath all the stressing surface things. The Real Thing is God's grace to the shattered human, the poor guy who's been done to death by the Law. Matt Johnson has lived this hopeful story. He's funny and honest and true."

> **Paul Zahl,** Retired Episcopal minister; former Dean/President of Trinity Episcopal School for Ministry in Pittsburgh; author of ten books

"For a relatively young author, Johnson reflects a rare spiritual maturity. He writes as one who has found new hope after spiritual fatigue, having been being tricked over and over again by communities and movements that advertised their commitment to good news but end up saddling followers with burdens neither our ancestors nor we could bear. He does this with a refreshing, candid, but never gimmicky style. Many who've been part of the American Christian experience will find his story familiar. For those who don't, it offers helpful insight into how many people from the author's generation have experienced Christianity in our times. In exposing the many forms 'latent theology of glory tendencies' can take, he's neither snarky nor condescending; rather, he invites us to join him in an exercise of self-assessment, and a journey to the foot of the cross. I recommend this book to anyone seeking restoration after being worn down by law-based religion."

Jeff Mallinson, Professor of Theology and Philosophy, Concordia University; cohost of *Virtue in the Wasteland*, a podcast; author of the forthcoming book, *Sexy: The Quest for Erotic Virtue in Perplexing Times*

"In his excellent, easy-to-read book *Getting Jesus Wrong*, Matt Johnson has outlined many of the pitfalls of evangelicalism and the draw of our hearts toward false Jesuses. I identified with each one and the despair that came with believing in them. I highly recommend sitting down with Matt for awhile and thinking through the biblical Jesus—you are going to find some good news here."

Marci Preheim, Author of *Grace Is Free, One Woman's Journey from Fundamentalism to Failure to Faith*

"I've known Matt for nearly twenty years and have always enjoyed his intelligence, perspective, and sincerity. We've shared shoddy stages, stinky vans, hacky podcasts, and many, many hours of conversation. That being said, two things stand out for me after reading *Getting Jesus Wrong*: 1) Matt's a better writer than I am, and 2) For all he knows, he has no idea how timely and needed this was for me. So much joy in remembering that . . . it IS finished. Enjoy!"

Mark Salomon, Author of *Simplicity*; vocalist for the bands Stavesacre, The Crucified, and White Lighter; host of the *Never Was* podcast

"I met Jesus twenty years ago and, to be honest, I've gotten Jesus wrong more times than I care to admit. The reasons are either bad teaching that I received or projecting my own ideas onto him. My friend Matt has written something that I wish I would've read early on in my faith, as it would've steered me in a far more biblical direction."

Alex Early, Pastor of Preaching & Theology, Redemption Church, Seattle, WA; author of *The Reckless Love of God* and *The New Believer's Guide to the Christian Life*

"Reading Matt's manuscript out loud to my husband as we drove cross country, there were long pauses as Matt's well-written words resonated. Too many times we were forced to agree . . . 'that's us.' Matt's transparent sharing about how often he got it wrong about Jesus, all in light of a church failure that broke a good many hearts, are wise words to ponder. As the saying goes, wisdom is learning from others' mistakes. Thanks, Matt, for your efforts to make us wise!"

Judy Dabler, Founder of Creative Conciliation

"*Getting Jesus Wrong* speaks directly and honestly to those who can no longer ignore or participate in the structures and systems that prioritize the control and conformity of the law over the freedom of the gospel. This book is funny and personal, as well as theologically rich. Author Matt Johnson's transparency about his own failures lends both credibility and insight into how the law and gospel interact in all of our lives."

Matt Carter, Founding member of the band Emery; cohost of *The Bad Christian* podcast

"What kind of 'Jesus' do you believe in? Is he the Jesus you and others around you have imagined for your own life stories? Or is he the radical Savior-King who messes up your life and saves you—really saves you, not only from his judgment but from yourself? This is a fun book to read. More than that, it's spot-on, filled with the Bible's central message. Tired of chicken-soup-for-the-soul spirituality? Then read this book!"

Michael Horton, Professor of Theology, Westminster Seminary California; cohost, *White Horse Inn* broadcast/podcast

"We live in an age when people aren't so much interested in what is true as they are in what works. And to their minds, what doesn't work is the boring same-old-same-old story of Jesus, God's perfect Son who fulfilled all the Law in our place, died the death we all deserve, and then rose to new life again, so that we can know we're lovingly forgiven, adopted, and cherished. Because we've yawned at the gospel, Jesus has been refashioned into a person who offers more practical help: he's given to you so that you can love yourself more, be a really great you, and be part of our really great movement. Matt Johnson struggled under the tyrant of that sort of Jesus until he discovered the wonder of the real Jesus—the One who dispenses both Law and Gospel. This book is a strong antidote to all the 'wrong' Jesuses out there. I encourage you to read it and share it with friends. You'll be glad you did."

Elyse M. Fitzpatrick, Author of *Because He Loves Me*

"Apparently it was Voltaire who originally quipped that 'In the beginning God created man in his own image, and ever since, man has been trying to repay the favor.' What sounds like a clever witticism is actually a devastating truism, the all-too-real consequences of which Matt Johnson unpacks here with both courage and a great sense of humor. *Getting Jesus*

Wrong is a terrific—dare I say, 'glorious'!—resource for anyone who's ever thought about (let alone believed in) Jesus, and one that I plan to hand out with abandon.

David Zahl, Editor of *The Mockingbird Blog*; author of *A Mess of Help*; coauthor of *Law And Gospel*

GETTING JESUS WRONG

Giving Up Spiritual Vitamins and Checklist Christianity

Matt Johnson

New
Growth
Press

WWW.NEWGROWTHPRESS.COM

New Growth Press, Greensboro, NC 27404
www.newgrowthpress.com

Cover Design: Faceout Studio, faceoutstudio.com
Typesetting and eBook: Lisa Parnell, lparnell.com

ISBN 978-1-942572-93-0 (Print)
ISBN 978-1-942572-94-7 (eBook)

Library of Congress Cataloging-in-Publication Data
Names: Johnson, Matt, 1972- author.
Title: Getting Jesus wrong : giving up spiritual vitamins and check-
list
  Christianity / Matt Johnson.
Description: Greensboro, NC : New Growth Press, 2017. | Includes
  bibliographical references and index.
Identifiers: LCCN 2016054896 | ISBN 9781942572930 (trade paper)
Subjects: LCSH: Christian life. | Jesus Christ--Person and offices.
Classification: LCC BV4501.3 .J634655 2017 | DDC 248.4--dc23
LC record available at https://lccn.loc.gov/2016054896

Printed in the United States of America
24 23 22 21 20 19 18 17   1 2 3 4 5

Contents

Preface

Years ago, I was lucky enough to work with a small group of pastorally gifted men. We were ministering in a megachurch in the context of Redemption Groups, which is a groups-based recovery ministry of sorts. Each of us was regularly teaching curriculum in short classes and wrestling with how to creatively remind others of God's love and care for his people amidst the grind of sin and suffering.

My friend Mike Wilkerson had developed the group curriculum and written the Redemption book, and I'd recently shifted gears from another ministry focus to join the Redemption ministry. Justin Holcomb was new to our church, and for a time he was involved with the Redemption ministry. He brought a depth of theological insight that was invaluable to the entire Redemption ministry and to the teams he later worked with.

One night—I think it was my second Redemption ministry teaching ever—Justin briefly shared some theological trivia from a somewhat obscure treatise written by Martin Luther. It was the crescendo statement of Luther's 1518 Heidelberg Disputation: God's love does not find, but creates, that which is pleasing to it. That sounds like Yoda-talk, I know. But read it again, slowly if you have to, because that statement is solid gold.[1]

It was exactly what I needed to hear. That short theological quip whetted my appetite for more of the same goodness. A theological shift began in my thinking, and it came at a good time. I'd been intentionally shooing away a spiritual restlessness I'd felt for a while. Some might fairly call it cognitive dissonance. The Jesus being portrayed in our megachurch culture was beginning to feel more and more cartoonish and one-dimensional—as if Jesus were a sort of pop-culture guru building an empire by selling spiritual commodities to accessorize the American dream. This wasn't the Jesus I'd read about in the Bible. I don't know, maybe I'm just getting crankier with age . . .

During that same time, Mike, Justin, and our fellow pastor and friend James Noriega scrounged an occasional weekday evening together at a local medieval-themed pub to discuss, debate, and defend our theological convictions. This is where Martin Luther's theology of the cross took root in my thinking. Between swigs of malty-hoppy goodness and long rants, this book idea started taking shape. (Of course my original idea wasn't anything close to the book you're reading, but the theological nuts and bolts are the same.) The story of Jesus continued to burrow deeper into my gut, reminding me that the simultaneous ugliness and beauty of Christ's cross guarantees that nothing can separate us from the love of God.

What I've slowly begun to unpack and come to terms with since those evenings at the pub is feeling duped by each church I've attended since my conversion in high school. In fairness, it's not exactly the church's fault. There have been plenty of good-hearted truth tellers along the way. Lots of good Jesus-focused preaching and teaching. Maybe it wasn't the message I was hearing as much as how my heart filtered the message. It's a chicken and egg quandary, I suppose. Whatever the case— whether it was crummy teaching, my own self-involved heart, the cultural air we all breathe, or all of the above—I've believed for a long time that the Christian life is supposed to be like some sort of extreme life makeover. But really, it's Christ and him crucified. There's a big, fat, gloriously freeing difference between the two. With any luck, I hope I can prove that differ-ence to you in these pages.

So to Mike, Justin, and James: thanks for the beers, the good conversations, and for faithfully showing me Jesus. Thanks for hanging in there as we took turns throwing theo-logical paint on the wall to see if it would stick. Guess what? It stuck.

Acknowledgments

Many thanks to friends and colleagues who have served—sometimes unwittingly—as my idea midwives. Birthing is often ugly business, and accordingly, it's not possible to write a book solo. Sorry, sometimes only a graphic visual will do.

These trusted people's insights poked and prodded me to make the main thing the main thing. Unfortunately, some deserve my recognition whose names I'm doomed to forget. If I've snubbed you, I'm a chump, and I'm sorry.

Thanks to Barbara Juliani at New Growth Press who encouraged me to write as if I were inviting the reader on a journey. She gave me way more work than I signed up for. (Thanks?) What I discovered along the way is that I didn't just need a manuscript paint touch-up. Instead, a wrecking ball had to be used to tear it down to the studs so that it could be rebuilt from the foundation up. Barbara's coaching helped me recognize that. Thanks are also due to the entire New Growth Press team. Putting out books is no small task, and I appreciate the work that happens behind the scenes.

Thanks to my editor Lauren Larkin for her dogged insistence on clarity and her theological eagle eyes. As an editor myself, I have to say that I was nervous about getting the editorial help I needed with this project. I was happily surprised that Lauren was enlisted to help. She was the exact coach I needed to tidy up the many sloppy sections of my manuscript and kick around the weakling bits needing more muscle and guts. She also helped me "land the plane" on the last couple chapters when I was unsure what to write next.

Thanks to Mike Wilkerson who has been a true partner not only in friendship, ministry, and our mutual affection of Nordic heavy metal, but through this book-writing process. He knows firsthand what it takes to birth a book. He understands the pains, joys, sorrows, and frustrations of discovering the unfortunate need to wad up an idea and toss it in the trash, and then shuffle back to the drawing board. During an impossibly demanding chunk of his own life, Mike made time for me—even if it was during the ten minutes he waited in line at the bank—to kick ideas around. Undoubtedly, Mike has helped me to craft this book in ways I'm likely unaware of.

Thanks to Justin Holcomb for the theological resources he passed on that have continued to haunt me. He encouraged me years ago to make this project happen and introduced my original book idea to the Key Life team.

Also, thanks to the many friends who have hung in there with me as I've strained to communicate with clarity. These many off-the-cuff conversations have helped craft every page. Thanks to Andy Maier, whose imagery of a guy getting pushed out a window strangely helped me focus my thoughts. To Joel Heflin, one of the few who looked over my proposal and sample chapters and provided feedback over tater tots and brews. To Colin and Lauren Day, who have always entertained my theological rants and given true, creative feedback on book cover design and potential titles. Also, thanks to Ryan Kearns, who showed kind interest in my project and helped me riff on metaphors over barbecue.

The most thanks goes to my wife Rose. She (and our sweet little girls) took the brunt of my everyday absentmindedness as I wrote amidst the most grueling yet meaningful years of our decade and a half together and as I worked on this longer than either of us anticipated. She taught me that an idea isn't full until it comes from the whole person. She helped me grab my idea from the stratosphere and yank it back down to earth so I could put my heart to the task of writing instead of just my brain. Thank you, and I love you.

The Problem

"And he asked them, 'But who do you say that I am?' Peter answered him, 'You are the Christ.'" (Mark 8:29)

"Philip said to him, 'Lord, show us the Father, and it is enough for us.'" (John 14:8)

Writing this book has been surprising. I hadn't set sail for self-discovery, but here's what I found: I'm a crappy Christian. Not only that, but the life of faith often does not feel good. Or fulfilling. I don't know, maybe I'm doing it wrong. In reality, I'm probably a much better pagan than a follower of Jesus. And how about you? Don't be shy. It's OK to admit it; this may be the open door to getting free of a stifling religion. So you're a crappy Christian. Don't worry; there's a Savior for that.

Writing a book is like rolling a giant rock up a hill. Outlining, editing, going on an archaeological dig for descriptive words—it's all part of sweating it out. Once gravity takes over, the rock bowls you over and you have to start all over again. The part where I discovered I was really a pagan (instead of the excellent Christian that could tell you how to get it right) just added insult to injury. You see, I set out to write a snarky spiritual corrective to all y'all's *bad* theology. I know. Pretty judge-y, right? Since all you nitwits out there believe wrongly, I was going to set the record straight. Turns out, I'm the nitwit.

I hadn't really planned to share personal stories through-out this exercise. I'd rather flex some spiritual brain muscles with the hope that you'd notice my bulging intellect. But as I began telling stories, I realized I wasn't choosing how this book would be written; it was being chosen for me. And that meant I couldn't put my best foot forward.

I realize now that during my twenty-five-plus years as a follower of Jesus, I've had many ideas about him. I've chased movements and given my best shot at checking off discipleship lists. I've tried to be good, and I've been where the exciting Christian movements are happening. The problem all along was that as part of these ideas, I've always thought of Jesus as a sort of lucky rabbit's foot. I wanted him to give me answers from the owner's manual for life.

When I consider the last decade and a half, I've thought of Jesus as a life coach, as the deity who handed me a moral checklist, as a movement leader who was inviting me to become great by my association with him. He was a visionary leader with a brilliant plan to homogenize culture. Between you and me, I was using God for his gifts rather than loving him as *The* Giver. I was using god stuff (formulas for creat-ing movements, personal discipleship programs, becoming an insider of an influential church) to ensure positive outcomes for my life. And all of that is a pagan enterprise.

Perhaps you've done similar things. Maybe you haven't had the same sorts of experiences I've had. You haven't been part of a "movement." You've never church hopped to chase the next exciting trend. But there is a pervasive, underlying mes-sage in many churches regardless of their theological flavor. And that message is basically, *you get what you give, good things happen to good people, and bad things happen to bad people.* Often churches have prescribed forms of "How to Live the Good Christian Life." It could be a discipleship program or a devotional practice. It may even be taking up the cause of the poor or marginalized. These are all great things, to be sure. But don't we often leverage these things in our hearts to ensure that we've got enough in our personal virtue account? Are these things meant to buy us that get-out-of-jail-free card?

The truth is that trouble still invades our lives. And when trouble comes, of course we feel let down and depressed, but somehow our belief that being a Christian meant a life without trouble makes our burdens even heavier. Now we have guilt (why can't I face this trouble with a laid-back faith?), shame (perhaps this trouble is my fault; if only I had been a better Christian), and of course anger (at ourselves, God, the churches we attended, and the leaders we followed). As for me, I'm done pretending life shouldn't hurt. Hope and healing come when we get to a place where we can truthfully admit what our real struggles are.

Often the brand of religion we've associated with has told us to follow our hearts and that our faith would feel like every day was a day at the spa. When real life catches up, we're left scratching our heads. This is not what we signed up for. May I ask you a question? What's more common among human beings: success and mountaintop experiences? Or struggle, hardship, and pain?

Last I checked, mortality rates are holding steady at 100 percent and entropy is still a scientific fact. I know that sounds more like something Eeyore would say than motivational guru Tony Robbins, but we are better off coming to terms with the facts of entropy. For years my idea of being religious was taking my spiritual vitamins so life would be better.[1] What were those vitamins? Pray harder. Devote yourself more wholeheartedly. Give to the ministry! Volunteer! But this is self-help, not salvation.

While we still live in a messed-up world, hope is not something we can activate through spiritual activity or church associations. No, the core of the Christian faith is about objective hope that lives outside of our personal experiences and hearts. Objective hope is found in the miracle of the death and resurrection of Jesus.

The self-help brand of Christianity has a fatal flaw: hope for life is supposed to be found in what believers actualize for themselves. We hear these catchphrases all the time: "Find the hope within," "Reach for the stars," "Never give up on your dreams," and the list goes on. The problem is that slapping these slogans onto Christianity doesn't work. Because the core of Christianity is the story of a Savior that . . . well . . . saves! The gospel is *not* a coach giving spiritual advice.

Unfortunately, the human heart has a default mode that mucks up our spirituality. As John Calvin has said, "The human mind is, so to speak, a perpetual forge of idols."[2] In the words of Brennan Manning, "It is always true to some extent that we make our images of God. It is even truer that our image of God makes us."[3] So often we project our hopes and dreams onto the divine will and then remake and rename our Savior. I'm guilty as charged.

In the coming chapters I'll give snapshots of a few of these false saviors: Jesus as Life Coach, Jesus as the Giver of the Moral Checklist, Jesus the Movement Leader, or the Visionary. Maybe these Jesuses have been my false saviors, but yours have been others. Maybe we can find some common ground.

I became a follower of Jesus at the age of sixteen, and my first church home was a little Pentecostal church. In this church, I was supposed to be a good boy; I wasn't. In my twenties, I attended a Calvary Chapel that said the same stuff, so I hid. I still wasn't good. Until a few years ago, I was part of a "cutting edge" church that, during a near twenty-year period, helped forge an influential brand within neo-reformed evangelicalism and was on the forefront of a church-planting movement. But then it flamed out just shy of the twenty-year mark, due in large part to the corrosive effects of the megalomania of its leadership and congregation. I could blame the higher-ups in leadership, but it was people like me that gave them a platform in the first place.

Each church experience shares a common thread: I was chasing after a movement of the spirit in an effort to normalize and capture a significant moment—a moment of excitement over church growth or cultural influence. Maybe there's a better way of putting it: I was chasing after an image I'd projected onto God. Turns out, that image was stick and carrot. And the stick and carrot inevitably lead to the cliff's edge of pride and despair.

Since I've come to terms with the stick and carrot of this false image of God, I've discovered the way out of the vicious cycle: death and resurrection. By death I mean both the little "d" deaths we experience throughout life and the inevitable big "D" death. This may all sound a little too cranky and dark. For the record, I do believe that belonging to Jesus makes a positive day-to-day difference in the lives of believers. But we simply can't expect life to be a string of mountaintop experiences. Expecting these types of experiences is corrosive to our souls because much of life is lived in a valley.

The bored, fickle human heart is always on the prowl to latch onto what's new and exciting. These same impulses are common among Christians. We want some kind of tactile proof that the Christian faith "works" and can deliver personal transformation so we can boast of our spiritual feats, apart from Christ. Well, we're in good company. Even Jesus's disciples—the twelve men who had spent three years with him—continually missed the point of who he was and what he was up to. They wanted a king to overthrow the Romans and restore their people to cultural, political, and religious significance. They thought they needed a powerful military leader unafraid of storming the castle. Instead, they got a Savior who died on a cross.

Think of the transfiguration account in Matthew 17:1–9. Jesus ascended a mountain and took James, John, and Peter along with him. Moses and Elijah appeared, and there was a spectacular Holy Ghost light show. Peter was overcome by the moment and said, "Lord, it is good that we are here. If you wish, I will make three tents here, one for you and one for Moses and one for Elijah" (verse 4). Like Peter, we long to hold on to a glorified image of life (all made possible by Jesus, of course). We long to make permanent the fleeting moments of glory. But as we scramble to capture the glory moment, we have this way of co-opting it. Rather than worship the glorious one, like Peter we imagine the side benefit we'll glean for ourselves. But notice that Peter's mountaintop experience came as a surprise—it wasn't a repeatable experience.

Likewise, experiences of glory we have in our own lives don't last long, and soon the regular rhythms of life demand us to come down off the mountain and walk the normal paths of life again, where we get dirty.[4] This glory moment wasn't something Peter could domesticate, duplicate, or hang on to, and neither can we.

Of course, this impulse to cling to mountaintop experiences is not new. As Martin Luther, the sixteenth-century church reformer, so aptly put it, in all our spiritual aspirations, we become theologians of glory.[5] That is, human beings have to ultimately see themselves as "doer and maker."[6] We need God's help, of course, but we are the ones to finally enact the principles, morals, or qualities God has given us. We human beings

> . . . find that putting [our] faith in the promises of God alone is too unsatisfying and too risky. It is like putting all their eggs in one basket. This is not to say that God cannot be involved or part of the picture. But we want to minimize the risk, and so we want to keep one hand on the wheel, or have a backup system in place, to be a part of a cooperative partnership where we rely partly on God and partly on ourselves. This would allow us to exercise a certain amount of control over our own destiny . . . these attempts [are called] "theologies of glory," in which human deeds elicit and thus predict (at least in part) God's deeds.[7]

We tend to see life as an upward progressing journey from one spiritual mountaintop to another, even where our successes in life are actually God's favor toward us. We love this narrative of progressing upward, our culture celebrates it, and many of our churches feed it. In hindsight, I've come to find in my own life that Luther's description of the glory story is what framed all my past churchly pursuits. The glory story comes in many forms, but it has one common denominator: it ascribes the very best of who we see ourselves to be, or the aspirations we believe that God has for us, and projects them back onto God.

We fashion our own ideas of who God is. Each of us is prone to our own biases and ideas of God's program for our lives in ways—the biases and ideas we most identify with. Take a closer look at kitschy images of Jesus, and it becomes clear that we often worship a savior of our own imaginations and personal preferences. Not only you—I'm included in the "we."

Consider that Jesus is a real flesh and blood human being who had preferences while he lived on earth, just as each of us does. Did he like his steak cooked well-done or rare? Would he have preferred paper or plastic at the checkout line? Is Jesus generally more conservative or generally more liberal? If Jesus were here in the flesh right now, would he tend to agree more with broadcast commentators on NPR or Fox? As it turns out, folks on opposing sides of the political fence all claim Jesus as their own. In 2012, a scholarly study came out that attempted to answer how Christians can come to such opposing conclusions when they look at political issues through the eyes of their faith. The basic gist of the study was that Christians characterize Jesus in their own image and project their politics and priorities onto the divine will.[8]

Beyond political perspective, consider personality traits like whether Jesus trends more as an introvert or extrovert. As for whether Jesus prefers evenings at home curled up with a book by the fire or whether he's always on the lookout for the hottest party spot, well, it really depends on your temperament. One well-known Christian professor and author actually gives his students a simple psychological test that asks questions like "Is Jesus a worrier?" Later in the text it asks similar questions, like "Are you a worrier?" The test reveals that with a large enough sample, we all think Jesus is a whole lot like we are.[9]

Compare this with the type of Christian leaders you respect. Some identify with mild-mannered, sagely but well-spoken leaders with good bedside manner who are focused on social justice. Others identify with influential, aggressive, culturally savvy movers and shakers. In 2010, the *New York Times* ran an article about an up-and-coming trend among young evangelicals using their interest in mixed martial arts fighting as a tool for evangelism.[10]

> John Renken is a pastor and a member of a fight team called Xtreme Ministries, a small church near Nashville that doubles as a mixed martial arts academy. Mr. Renken, who founded the church and academy, doubles as the team's coach. The school's motto is "Where Feet, Fist, and Faith Collide." (Now if that's not a perfect faith-infused Jackie Chan movie title, I don't know what is.) Mr. Renken's ministry is one of a small but growing number of evangelical churches that have embraced mixed martial arts—a sport with a reputation for violence and blood that combines kickboxing, wrestling, and other fighting styles—to reach and convert young men, whose church attendance has been persistently low. Mixed martial arts events have drawn millions of television viewers, and one was the top pay-per-view event in 2009.
>
> Recruitment efforts at the churches, which are predominantly white, involve fight night television viewing parties and lectures that use ultimate fighting to explain how Christ fought for what he believed. Other ministers go further, hosting or participating in live events.

The goal, these pastors say, is to inject some machismo into their ministries—and into the image of Jesus—in the hope of making Christianity more appealing. "Compassion and love—we agree with all that stuff, too," said Brandon Beals, the lead pastor at Canyon Creek Church outside of Seattle. *"But what led me to find Christ was that Jesus was a fighter"*[11](emphasis mine).

Beals's quote says it all. The Jesus he identified with was a fighter, just like him.

Everyone has an image of Jesus they prefer, a Jesus who values what they value: Tough-guy Jesus, Wise Sage Jesus, Bearded, Tattooed, Skinny Jeans Jesus, Khakis and Polo Shirt Jesus, Suit and Tie Conservative Jesus, or Social Revolutionary Jesus. On a deeper level, our personal images of Jesus reveal that we think the Christian faith is about furthering our hopes and dreams, and that Jesus is the primary catalyst for getting us where we want to be in life. This is another way of saying, in the words of Gerhard Forde, we all are "inveterate theologians of glory."[12] When we operate within the glory-story paradigm, it reveals we're in love with all the attractiveness of power, influence, success, or possessions, and we call it being "blessed."[13] We're encouraged by all the cliché slogans "reach for the stars" and "don't give up on your dreams," but then like a flaky boyfriend or girlfriend, when we don't "feel the chemistry" anymore, when real life really falls apart, suddenly our relationship with Jesus is on shaky ground.[14]

But Jesus didn't set up shop on that mountain with Peter, and he didn't intend for us to live there either. God works in ways that are the opposite of our lofty imaginings. If we take the story of Jesus at bare-bones face value, he wasn't a great success. God sent Jesus into the world to be born in a barn. He was born into scandal (imagine the naysayers: "Yeah, right, Mary conceived of the 'Holy Spirit'"), he worked a regular job, he didn't study under a famous Rabbi, he claimed he was God, many people thought he was crazy or demon possessed, and he was executed like a criminal. In our day and age where only good things in life constitute being blessed, it would seem that Jesus was anything but.

It's only by faith that we can grasp that God reveals his character on the cross. On the cross, God subverted everything we intuitively understand about power. "Of all the places to search for God, the last place most people would think to look is the gallows."[15] Instead of demanding power for himself and presenting himself as a God who ". . . could knock heads and straighten people out when they got out of line . . . ,"[16] God, in Christ, laid down his power and died for us.

But for many of us, coming to terms with the thought that great blessings come through great suffering is a tough pill to swallow.[17] Reformed church historian Carl Trueman recalls giving a talk on Martin Luther's theology of the cross and the pushback he received from a listener in attendance. "I was challenged afterwards by an individual who said that Luther's theology of the cross did not give enough weight to the fact that the cross and resurrection marked the start of the reversal of the curse, and that great blessings should thus be expected; to focus on suffering and weakness was therefore to miss the eschatological significance of Christ's ministry."[18]

It's most certainly true that we are blessed on account of Jesus, but that blessing is not yet fully realized in the now—it is a future hope that we cling to in the uncertain present. Not because Jesus hasn't done it all yet—he has. The cross is a historical event, and it has ramifications for the present. We have been justified, we are being justified, and we will be justified. At the same time, the cross is also the pattern of the Christian life where he meets us in death before he resurrects us back to life. He meets us not only in our final death, but the little deaths of life along the way—our struggles, failures, and sufferings in this world.

Jesus has already had his Easter (his bodily resurrection), but we're still waiting for our final Easter. That is, we still have to die and be resurrected. We live our lives in the shadow of the cross, awaiting his glorious return, and we live with the assurance that when we die in him, we are also raised in him.[19]

We don't need a faith that will make all our dreams come true as we set up camp on our mountaintop. We need a faith strong enough to handle the weight of our own death. Not just our final resting place death, but all the little deaths along the way. When work dries up or the scholarship doesn't come through, when our spouse walks away from a marriage, or a dangerous habit threatens to engulf our lives, we need a hope stronger than a God-sponsored optimism because when it comes down to it, we can't seem to live up to our own standards, and sometimes our dreams become nightmares. We need a sure hope beyond ourselves. But we seem to have endless ways of fooling ourselves with false hopes.[20] Thankfully,

> true hope, the kind of trust that will not let you down in the end, will have to go against what your eyes have become accustomed to loving. You are addicted to placing your hope in whatever appeals to you, and then love and hope get terribly entangled. In that case, making the proper distinction in order to get hope right is very hard. You fall in love with what your eyes see, and that is only the surface stuff—the slick, glitter, momentary appeal of a thing. Or what is even more dangerous, you start loving your highest morals, goals, and ideals. "Set your goals." "Never give up." "Don't let anyone take away your dreams." Those are all slogans meant to prop up the world's faltering hopes in dying gods.[21]

But true hope rejects Jesus as life coach, guru, or cosmic vending machine. Instead, real, true, and lasting hope embraces that which we can't always see. It goes beyond "don't give up on your dreams" and what our eyes see, otherwise it's no hope at all.[22]

The mountaintop that your heart, culture, or some leader has called you to may not exist. Worse yet, rather than a mountaintop, it may turn out to be a valley, or a flaming brown paper bag full of dog doo-doo left on the front porch of your already burnt-down house. These times of life are never what we sign up for, and they clash with our ideas of what we think a proper spiritual life ought to look like. While our loves and hopes are always directed toward the attractive and good, God's love is directed toward what is unattractive: us. We love things in life because they're beautiful to us. But we're beautiful to God *because* he loves us. There's a huge difference.

Here's another reason why the Jesus of the mountaintop is no good for you, or for the church. If the mountaintop is supposed to be normative, those in the spiritual valley are out of luck. They will have to climb back up on the mountain so they can have assurance that God is really with them and makes a "real" difference in their life. But what happens when your body seizes up from exhaustion, you're out of breath, and you can't climb one more step? That's not hope, that's just a tragically missed opportunity. You weren't strong enough. Tough luck.

Here's the good news: the mountaintop experiences of life aren't normative. If everything in our lives of faith were a mountaintop, then nothing would be a mountaintop. Jesus does not require that we ascend up to him; he descends to us (Deuteronomy 30:12–13). Following Jesus may include occasional mountaintop experiences in life, but most of the time, just like the disciples, we follow him through the highways and byways of life, and our feet get tired, blistered, and really dirty. But when the journey is too much, when we're down for the count, Jesus does not whip us into submission. He tends to our wounds. He shows mercy and compassion in our failure.

So come along with me on this journey. I'm going to introduce you to some old friends. Well, specters, really—the false ideas of Jesus that have haunted me and caused me a good bit of trouble, come to think of it. Each version of Jesus held out blessings and never quite delivered. At times the culture was to blame. Sometimes it was a crummy preacher. Often it was my own heart. And still my Savior—my real Savior—has hunted me down. When he caught me, he told me something unexpected: death is part of the deal, but it's not the last word because he is the resurrection and the life (John 11:25–26a).

In telling stories, my hope is that you'll connect the dots to your own disappointments and pains. Telling stories, naming things—it helps. It doesn't always make circumstances better, but I've found it helps me feel less isolated. Or crazy.

We'll do a tad bit of theology, and I'll try not to be a bore about it. We'll try and keep our heads out of the clouds and down on the ground where real life happens. In the process maybe we can learn a shared vocabulary that will help us make sense of some things.

As we go about this task, I am keenly aware of the possibility of "getting Jesus wrong" all over again. It's possible (probably inevitable) that a decade or two removed from now, I'll find ideas and theologies in these pages that are "wrong." Ah, well. We'll do the best we can, keeping an awareness that our faith matures along the way. But on each step of the way faith must be grounded in who Jesus is and what he's done. By faith we see what he's doing in the present by his Spirit, and we see the future hope that awaits us.

I'll tell some irreverent jokes along the way. It's true. We Christians can buy into some pretty dumb things sometimes. It's OK to laugh about it. And if you don't mind, I may have to do a bit of personal lamenting as well. Misery loves company, so feel free to join me. I suppose this is natural, given that I've had some wrong-headed ideas about things for two and a half decades.

So we'll poke fun, have our laughs, maybe even cry a bit. Or we'll take our time and repent of our old ways. Maybe you'll find out you're a crappy Christian just like me. Maybe it's time to admit the life of faith doesn't always feel like a party. But I sincerely hope you find . . . hope. Not hope in what is in your heart for God, but what is in God's heart for you.[23] Not hope in what you must do for God, but in what your Savior has already done for you. Hope that in the little "d" deaths of life, even the big "D" death, at the end of it all, he'll answer it with resurrection. Because resurrection is all we've got.

Part I

Life Coach Jesus and Other False Gods

Chapter 1
Life Coach Jesus

WHAT DO YOU WANT FROM JESUS?

If you were face-to-face with Jesus and he asked you, "What do you want from me?" what would you say? Some of us would like tips for living successfully or being fulfilled. Some of us might like him to snap his fingers and make our troubles disappear or do a magic trick, some sort of miracle. Maybe you're deeper than I am and concerned about the ills of the world. Maybe you'd ask Jesus for world peace or the end of hunger. Just like those who interacted with him two thousand years ago, we all want something from Jesus.

And it makes sense that drawing near to the Son of God would mean, at least in part, that life would work the way it should—that our life stories would reflect properly working lives. Our stories would be the kind that include healthy bodies, flourishing relationships, and babies in far-off countries getting fed. After all, Jesus said, I've come to give you abundant life (John 10:10).

But as any Christian knows, belonging to Jesus doesn't mean all is right with the world—or our personal lives. When real life smacks up against these kinds of statements from Jesus, we scratch our heads wondering what Jesus meant. How does getting a pink slip from your boss, or finding out you have gallstones, or hearing about the sudden death of a family member equal abundant life? We expect that following Jesus somehow means all the pieces of life will fall into place—or that life will improve over time. The truth is that it doesn't always go that way.

Let me pose the question again. Imagine sitting across from Jesus at a table, and he asks you—non-threateningly and without an ounce of condescension, with honest and kind eyes and with care—"what would you like me to do for you?" The religious-minded answers are fairly predictable: "I just want to be in your presence," "I just want to know you better." But in day-to-day reality, our lives say something different. At least mine does.

POSITIVE MENTAL ATTITUDE, FREE ENTERPRISE, AND GROWING UP "CHRISTIAN-Y"

I've often been asked, "Did you grow up in a Christian home?" I'm not always sure how to answer the question. My dad grew up Catholic, and my mom was a burnt-out Methodist. When they got married, as the story goes, my mom begrudgingly went to Catholic catechism. We went to church with grandparents once or twice a year. Usually it was a Christmas Eve candlelight service. I loved it as a kid. It meant I got to play with fire in a controlled environment. Other than the annual pyrotechnics of Christmas Eve, religion consisted of recited dinnertime prayers. (To this day I can't remember the words until I'm around the table and Dad starts with the first syllable. Then I can chant the entire thing along with the rest of the family. Vocal muscle memory, I guess.) So mealtime prayers and candlelight Christmas Eve services with the grandparents was the extent of religion in our home. General belief in God? Yes. I knew Jesus was important, but I hadn't put the whole picture together yet. Then Dad joined Amway.

At the mere mention of Amway, some people scoff and imagine a schlocky pyramid scheme meant to bait people into buying household products. But I can say with all sincerity that Amway played an important role in our family for a couple years. I was only in grade school when Dad joined "the biz." My dad was a public school music teacher (a darn good one) for his entire career, and in case you didn't know, that shouldn't be your career of choice if you're planning to buy a vacation house in the Florida Keys. So we lived on very little, and I respect my dad for mustering the courage to become a salesman for the sake of earning extra cash for our family.

There's a whole lot that could be said about Amway, but having a positive mental attitude was basically one of the Ten Commandments. Whatever your circumstances in life, if you would not or could not think positively, you weren't going to get anywhere in life. Another thing that went hand in hand with Amway was Jesus. There were a lot of really successful people in Amway who were fired-up, born-again, turbo Christians. Though faith wasn't a prerequisite to be in the business, it was definitely a part of the culture. So when I was around ten or eleven, out of the blue, Dad started taking us to church. If you wanted to be a success, make a lot of money, and do something worthwhile with your life, you needed to get Jesus and have a can-do attitude. Jesus and positive mental attitude went hand in hand.

P.M.A. with a Mohawk

Fast-forward a couple years. I'm your classic smart-aleck teenager with very average grades who thinks the school principal has a targeted, diabolical plan to ruin my life. I'm into skateboarding, punk rock, and I've got an attitude to match. Isn't that half of the male teenaged population, even today? Yeah, I was a real "individual." For the most part, I didn't get into much trouble. I had some sketchy friends, but I made it through junior and senior high school relatively unscathed.

My sophomore year, my older sister—who'd recently had a radical conversion—was home for a visit, and she was evangelizing our entire family: my two older brothers, my mom and dad, and me. She was persuasive, and I was convicted. I believed in Jesus, but until then, I didn't want to obey him. The religious shorthand for what happened next is "I got saved." I became a Christian. I prayed the prayer, started reading my Bible, and went to church.

There were hurdles though. Christians were in no way cool. This is a pretty big deal as a teenager. The skateboarding/ music scene was my life at that point, and it didn't go together real well with Jesus. Christians were so straight laced, and buttoned down. So . . . I dunno, *holy*. No smoking and drinking, and in some cases, no rock and roll. Fortunately for me, I found something special: Straightedge Hardcore. Straightedge what-the-huh?

For those out of the loop, Straightedge Hardcore originated as a subculture in the 1980s punk rock scene in Washington, DC, with a band called Minor Threat. The particular genre and culture continued on over the years and is still going strong today, although the music genre has morphed many times. And in case you haven't heard, Straightedge Hardcore—bands like Youth of Today, Bold, and Gorilla Biscuits—sound like a runaway train threatening to veer off the tracks and destroy everything in its path and then add more guitars, screaming, and testosterone.

Imagine male teenaged angst turned up to ten with a morality code set to scathingly fast, unskilled Neanderthal music. The basic tenets of Straightedge promote clean living: don't drink, don't smoke, don't be sexually promiscuous. That's 1980s Straightedge.

One of the big ideas that came out of Straightedge was born in response to punk rock. Punk culture tended to be debauched and veered toward nihilism. The Straightedge mentality was an effort to be a constructive answer to that. Why not keep the intensity of the music and lifestyle, yet not be a bonehead by ruining your life with substance abuse?

Straightedge was a great companion to my newfound faith. After all, being a Christian meant personal holiness. And that meant no drinking, smoking, and going around with girls. Especially in the little Pentecostal church I was now part of.

Life Coach Jesus = A Happy Life or Running Laps until You Puke

What's the point of the above life snapshots? Jesus comes onto the scene of our lives within a particular context. He came into your context, and he came into mine as well. The context informs our understanding of who he is and how he changes our lives. My particular context centered around being a good person, thinking positively, and doing something of substance with my life. In the midst of this particular context, I encountered Jesus. The stories I share highlight this context.

None of the aspects of my context were particularly bad—a positive mental attitude and clean living were good things. This is the life compass you'd hope your new neighbors possess. The problem is that none of these good things can save you. I'd go so far as to say that envisioning the Christian life primarily about living right and achieving one's goals is miles away from what the Christian faith is really about. Why? Because that narrative makes the Christian faith about us and what we are doing, not about Christ and what he has done.

The Jesus I signed up to follow was a wise teacher, a moral reformer, a life coach that desired to help improve my life. This Jesus preaches a one-dimensional message: do the right thing, and when you do, you'll live a happy fulfilling life. Lucky me, I was the teacher's pet. It was a great message when my heart was inclined to do the right thing and when I had some will-power in the tank and was up for the challenges of life. But it was a bad message when I didn't want to be good—or *couldn't* be good. Then Life Coach Jesus will grind you into the ground and make you do laps until you vomit into the bushes.

Think about a coach's primary role. Coaches evaluate, ask how you're doing on the path to achieving your goals, help you with tips to keep you on track, and occasionally cheer with some motivational talk. If you're not doing well or you're not hitting your goal, your coach is going to be your worst enemy. And yet at the end of the day, whether you're on the coach's good side or not, the results are up to you and you have to want it. The coach is there to help you become your best, to help you write your own life story. Notice the commonality here, and observe the object of the emphasis: you.

DOES GOD EXIST TO MAKE OUR LIVES BETTER?

If nothing else, Christianity is about—wait for it—Jesus, not you or me. It's about Jesus acting for our good by living, dying, and rising for us. And Christianity is (thankfully) about him in thousands of different ways—ways that I look forward to spending the rest of my life unpacking, and learning and drawing near to. I hope you do too. I don't imagine any Christian disagreeing with this. Of course the Christian faith is about Jesus. But *how* we perceive Jesus being at the center of our faith is at the crux of the kind of faith we have, and rightly or wrongly orients our faith.

In a 2005 study of American youth and how they view spirituality, sociologists Christian Smith and Melinda Lundquist Denton, coined a term that has gained popularity over the last decade. Smith and Lundquist Denton claim that across denominational lines there is a common spiritual belief among young people that characterizes them. Smith and Lundquist Denton summed up a generation's general spiritual beliefs in a term: Moralistic Therapeutic Deism (MTD).[1] If you've paid attention to culturally savvy Christian figures in recent years, you may have heard this term explained before. The basic ideas behind MTD include the following:

1. A god exists who created and ordered the world and watches over human life on earth.
2. God wants people to be good, nice, and fair to each other, as taught in the Bible and by most world religions.
3. The central goal of life is to be happy and to feel good about oneself.

4. God does not need to be particularly involved in one's life except when he is needed to resolve a problem.
5. Good people go to heaven when they die.

Honestly, this outlook pretty well sums up my beliefs as a teenager—maybe even into my twenties. Much ink has been spilled on this subject, and I don't have any new insights to add. But these findings seem to resonate far and wide, and I'd venture to say that this isn't just a general attitude of a younger generation, but ideas that seem to describe American spirituality in general.

If MTD is an accurate spiritual barometer, the logic of this belief is that God basically exists to make our lives better. Consider the times, though, when belief in God doesn't make things better. And when those experiences come, it either turns one inward—"I can't believe I messed this up, I know better..."— or toward God in accusation—"I thought God would protect me. Where is he now that life has gone down the toilet?"

Sad, Spiritual Moralism

Let's look at the "I can't believe I messed this up" response. This is what the sad, spiritual moralist sounds like.[2] The "sad, spiritual moralist" is the most reticent in giving up their blinders. These folks don't ordinarily deal with substance addiction or passed-out-in-the-gutter type of sin; rather, they suffer an addiction to their bad feelings over spiritual failure. This may sound jaded, but I have developed a keen sense for these folks and can spot them within minutes because I'm a sad, spiritual moralist myself. The sad, spiritual moralist sounds very humble, broken, and contrite to everyone else, but more often than not they are simply wallowing in pride.

In recent years I was involved in volunteer pastoral work and served as one of many leaders of a recovery group ministry. When it comes to the sad moralist, there are a lot of us out there. One young guy in particular comes to mind. This young man had grown up in a Christian household. In fact, his dad was a pastor. He struggled with drinking too much alcohol and viewing porn, but what really ate at him was his regret for having not made better life choices. "If only" he'd been more serious about his discipleship, "if only" he'd served more at the church, he'd be closer to God and have achieved something meaningful in his life.

Many of us can relate to his woes. We feel spiritually inept. We know what the right thing to do is, but we just can't seem to do it (Romans 7:15–25, anyone?). And often those of us who grew up in churches where we were served a steady diet of morality instead of forgiveness and grace don't know what to do about our feelings of spiritual ineptitude. There are many factors involved in why people lug guilt around. I am not saying it's wrong to be sad or depressed, especially as it pertains to sin in our lives. This is not a judgment as much as an observation.

In the story above, the young man seemed to be most concerned with failing himself. He'd considered himself a moral person of good pedigree. A pastor's kid with Bible knowledge who knew better than to allow for these sorts of moral failures and missed opportunities. I can't claim exact discernment on what was going on in that guy's heart and mind, but I sensed a struggle that was familiar in my own experience of internalizing guilt and shame—guilt and shame that starts playing in a continuous loop with no hope of resolve. You see, sin can't be reformed or polished. Sin can't get put back on the right track. No, sin isn't a problem we can solve through our hard work of spiritual introspection. Sin can't get fixed through introspection. Our sin is forgiven. And once we see the forgiveness Jesus gives, we're set free from trying to "figure it out" within ourselves.

Like I'm one to talk. "Figuring it out" has taken up a colossal amount of brainpower and heartache in my own life when times are hard. The need to "figure it out" has ultimately worn me down and caused me depression, relational strain, and a lot of unnecessary heartache.

Have you ever used an old computer that's bogged down and slow only to realize you have about fifty-two programs running in the background? Of course the computer's running slow. All the memory is eaten up with opened programs that aren't in use. You've got to close some tabs and shut some programs down so the computer will function as it should. That's a picture of my brain and heart—the computer with too many programs open trying to "figure out" every sin, failure, and internal motivation.

Of course we need to prayerfully engage in self-assessment. But don't do this alone. Invite a trusted friend or counselor into your world because introspection can turn bad when we become self-obsessed with our failings. Rather than "figure out" the problems, I've had to learn to grieve—grieve wrongs I've committed and those committed against me and grieve periods of time lost in relationship with others due to self-focus. We can't un-sin. That's like trying to put toothpaste back into a tube.[3] It's an impossible task. But you can grieve over failures, sins, and broken relationships. Grief is not a dead end. We can also face our Savior amidst our grief, knowing he grieves alongside us and we will never be turned away. Not ever. That's the daily, healing cycle of repentance, turning to Christ in faith, and believing in the forgiveness of sins.

When we don't turn to Jesus with our sins and sorrows, we stay stuck in grief-less cycles of guilt and shame. That's what comes natural to us. Try and convince a person who struggles with compulsive overeating not to think about food, or tell a woman who is insecure about her appearance to stop comparing herself to others, or try to get a drunk to just stop drinking. Likewise, it's almost impossible to get a sad, spiritual moralist to take their eyes off the impossible task of sorting through their spiritual rat's nest of a problem and look up and out toward their Savior. I know because I've been there.

Is More Life Coaching the Answer?

In order to get out of this impossible state, many of us turn toward (more) moralistic teaching to get a positive thinking pick-me-up. Gifted Christian speakers bearing these kinds of messages come along, and people praise how well they're able to make the Word "come alive" and make the Bible "relevant for today." They preach messages focused on solving common life problems while keeping a good attitude. They preach about saving and spending finances, keeping the spark alive in marriage, or staying positive when life's got you down.

I think I understand why people are drawn to this kind of preaching. Good Christian teaching will help us apply something helpful to our lives. I truly believe there's a place for that. On the other hand, when not done well, this kind of communication becomes mere Jesus-talk moralism that we can just as well get off a self-help bookshelf. The problem is, self-help doesn't seem to . . . help.

This kind of preaching might sound a little like the following:

> There is a seed within you trying to take root. That's God trying to get you to conceive. He's trying to fill you with so much hope and expectancy that the seed will grow and bring forth a tremendous harvest. It's your time. You may have been sick for a long time, but this is your time to get well. You may be bound by all kinds of addictions, all kinds of bad habits, but this is the time to be set free. You may be struggling financially, in all kinds of debt, but this is the time for promotion. This is your time for increase. Friend, if you will get in agreement with God, this can be the greatest time of your life. This can be the time that God pours out His immeasurable, far and beyond favor.[4]

It's my sincere hope that you are not influenced by this kind of toothy grinned, megachurch preacher kind of nonsense. In the end, it can't save you. It's life advice without living power. As an old friend once said to me, this kind of spirituality is great—that is, until you actually need it.

WHEN BEST INTENTIONS MEET REALITY

By age nineteen, I'd been a Christian for a few years. I'd faithfully attended church, read my Bible, and prayed regularly. I remember those few years fondly: I was learning more about the Bible, enjoying a sense of family within my church, and growing closer to my three older siblings as we attended church together. And I had Straightedge as my motivational soundtrack. I was going to live clean and honor God with my lifestyle. Then life struck.

I met a girl and we started dating. The problem was that we couldn't keep our hands off each other. I so prided myself on remaining pure until marriage. I was a "good Christian boy." You can guess what happens next. I can remember driving home one night after things had started to go too far physically. I bawled aloud, pounding on the dashboard, berating myself for my sin. I was angry and frustrated with myself. I knew better, and yet I was consciously sinning. Looking back, I don't think I was lamenting my sin against God or this woman. I was mostly disappointed in myself. I knew what was right, and yet I was doing all the wrong things. I'd failed my own moral code.

I'd said the sinner's prayer, and I was on the right track by attending church, reading my Bible, praying, and getting involved in Christian community. Yet, my life was miles away from what a model of the Christian life should be. In this particular instance, I prayed that God would help me be self-controlled and help me to root out sin in my life. I even half confessed to friends who I'd hoped would keep me accountable.

The problem was that they were all in the same boat in their relationships. The sad fact was that nothing worked. And I remained in an unhealthy on-again off-again relationship for nearly three years. I wasted her time and my own.

WE NEED A STORY BIGGER THAN OURSELVES

There's no way out for the sad moralist lamenting over failure to keep the rules, unless they're able to get out of the cycle of obsessing over checking their own spiritual temperature.[5] My recovery group participants and I all have something in common—we believe, much like one influenced by Moralistic Therapeutic Deism, that having God in your life "makes things better." And when the spiritual math doesn't add up, we often despair that our faith wasn't enough. In the end, Life Coach Jesus's tips for life didn't work, and we wound up guilty.

There's a better story line here. Rather than view the Christian life as an achievable game of morality and then fall into inevitable prideful despair aghast at our sin and our failure to live up to the rules, we can take our eyes off of our own navels and look up and out. This involves straightening up and looking to what Jesus has done in his historical, objective, living, dying, and rising *for us* (Romans 4:25) and holding on for dear life to his proclamation that "it is finished" (John 19:30). God's alternative story line is much richer, redemptive, and powerful than our own self-made story of morality-laden pat-a-cake. We need preachers to tell us an Exodus-like story—a story of a God who saves his people from oppressive evil, who creates a nation of people for himself and brings them through the wilderness to a promised land. We need the story of the Savior who willingly goes to his death for his enemies and is resurrected again for their freedom.

Our self-made stories of "God helps those who help themselves"[6] are a flaccid substitute to the true and eternal hope of God (not you or me) making all things new. Then he will bring us home to a place where he wipes away all tears, where death is no more, where there will be no more crying or pain (Revelation 21:1–8). God's hope is not condescending wishful thinking that comes to meet us halfway with an eye roll and big sigh so long as we do our part and "give it our best try." The strength of God's hope isn't wobbly-kneed. Instead, he drags us into eternity on a stretcher even if we've willingly traipsed through a moral minefield and come out the other side limbless. This is the sort of heavy, full, lasting, iron-spined hope we need preached to us, not the hollow ring of "do your best, God does the rest."

Adolescent me thought Christian identity was synonymous with exemplary moral living and achieving personal goals. But then, seemingly out of nowhere, life smacked me in the face, and my puny Life Coach Jesus was unable to do much for me but tell me to exercise more and get in spiritual shape. I was on my own with a handful of principles to live by, but the principles only pointed out my failure. I was weak. They didn't do anything to help me.

It would be convenient to say that the teenaged back-slidden version of me had been misled by a steady diet of wrongheaded messages from the pulpit. I'm not a Pentecostal or Charismatic anymore, but I do think my old pastor was preaching Jesus to me. It wasn't necessarily the mailman's error; there was also fault with the mail receiver. The impotent version of Jesus I was left with was something my own heart had conjured up. And that version of Jesus is insufferable and couldn't help me in time of need (and he's unable to help you either). Like working with a coach, all that's left is your stats, some tips for how to do better next time, and the pit in your stomach that you're not improving.

The sad, spiritual moralists I've had the privilege to counsel over the years have all needed a bigger story. The nineteen-year-old me—hopped up on hormones, deceit, and the anxiety-ridden inferiority complex I lugged into adulthood—needed a bigger story. You've got your own problems, and you need a bigger story too. I don't know about you, but I don't need a life coach; I need a Savior.

Chapter 2
Checklist Jesus

I am standing in front of a church congregation with a microphone in my hand. A spotlight is shining on my face, and there is a crowd of about two hundred people in front of me. I'd just been put on the spot by my pastor and had to come up with something to say with about thirty seconds to think about it. This is the stuff that nightmares are made of.

One of the last times I'd had to stand up in front of a large crowd was about twenty-plus years prior at a poetry recital. I'd memorized Shel Silverstein's, "Captain Hook" poem, won the class competition, and was supposed to recite the poem in front of the entire school. I looked out at the crowd, my mind went blank, and any memory of that poem magically evaporated out of my brain with a sea of searing eyeballs glaring at me. I didn't pee my pants, but I did cry and punch a giant stage curtain as I ran off the stage. Not my best grade-school moment.

Here I was faced with public speaking again, and fortunately, it didn't turn out as badly. But it was years later that I learned something about myself from that impromptu testimony. I'd unconsciously meant to flatter myself. And it wasn't very flattering.

At the time, I was attending a church where the pastor gave expositional sermons, which is a fancy way of saying he preached through entire books of the Bible word for word. If you've read the Bible for more than just a few minutes, you know there are bits in there that don't quite seem to be especially relevant for the here and now. We were in one of those sections, and in order to be faithful to the preaching form, our pastor was making the most of the passage in a creative way. He was preaching through one of the apostle Paul's letters where it's common for Paul to give closing remarks addressing specific friends who have helped him in his ministry travels. A hello here, a thank-you there, and the occasional please-bring-my-warm-coat-next-time-you-visit message. This is one of those sections that doesn't quite lend itself to practical application.

The pastor was creative with the passage, which I think the congregation appreciated. He used the passage as an opportunity to highlight people like me and say thank you for partnering with the church in ministry by volunteering time. It was my turn up at the mic, and the pastor said in effect, "Thanks for being here each week and volunteering your time and talents." Then he asked me to give a short testimony about when I came to the church and what was going on in my life at the time. Basically, this is what I said: "I came to the church during a confusing time in my life. I was struggling with theological and philosophical ideas and there were some people in the church who understood my questions and helped straighten me out."

Fast-forward about five years. I am on a stroll with my wife in a park on a spring day. The smell of new blooms is in the air, and the welcome sunshine is unfamiliar to our squinty eyes. Our conversation features a retrospective look at the last few years—the good times, the bad, and the things we've learned along the way. Something one of us said reaches into the cobwebs of my memory about that mini-testimony in front of the congregation. Instantly, I realize that pious little speech in front of the church all those years ago was not only Christless, but it was all about me.

The backstory to that mini-testimony is that over the course of about a ten-year stretch, I'd come out of a not-so-great—well, let's be honest—sinful time of my life. A few broken dating relationships were in the rearview mirror, and more than a few drunken nights wrapped up into a black hole pursuit of trying to earn a living in rock and roll. I'd gotten "straightened out" in a sense, but I had never truly faced my sin before my Savior. Instead, I'd accepted the counterfeit of theological study as a cover. It was the one thing that came natural to me, and also seemed like the spiritual thing to do. I was beginning to appreciate the depth and complexity of adult life, and I'd set out to crack some codes. In the process, I'd fallen for the subtle lie that knowledge of good Christian theology somehow served as a spiritual truce with God. I'd used a good thing (theological study) as a defense mechanism against authenticity. I'd thumbed my nose at the reality that I was a saved sinner who needed Jesus, just like everybody else.

THE DISCIPLINES THAT DRIVE US

As friends and family can attest, I live inside my head. I'm not sure I knew this about myself until I met my wife. After fifteen-plus years of life together, I've realized not everyone views the world as I do. Imagine that. Here's how my brain works: picture a giant funnel above your head and all of the data of life dumps in at the top. Past and present life experiences, pop culture, ideas from books, conversations—everything dumps into that funnel. Somewhere between those two ears an average brain is camping out and solving complex problems (at least I'd like to think they're complex). Out from the bottom of the small part of the funnel come very specific and important interests and truths. (At least I hope they're truths.)

I can't help but see connections everywhere, like threads pinned down by red thumbtacks on a map of the world and all tangled into an impossible web. When I can latch onto a concept that makes sense of the world through those disparate connections, I go with it. This is simply how my brain works to make sense of the world. When my feet hit the floor in the morning, I'm excited to learn and acquire knowledge. Ideas and systems of thought drive me.

These driving factors come in a variety of flavors. Many of the things that motivate us are positive, although when left unchecked and used for selfish gain, they can turn negative too. These driving factors might be achievement, a relationship, money, influence, power, a political cause, prestige, and surprise, surprise—in my case—religion. Our lives are full of these driving factors.

Most of us have peculiar things we naturally fixate on. Mastering a theological systematic (ahem, that'd be me), ensuring future security through an investment portfolio, raising up academically successful kids, trying to beat the clock through diet and exercise, protecting our reputations, or maybe it's just keeping an organized closet. We think if we could whip that *one thing* into shape, all of life would fall into place like a perfectly played Tetris game. We have checklists in our hearts and minds bent toward the things we long to conquer. And when we finally conquer those mountains, we'll enter a blissful life. I'm not sure I've thought of it consciously until recently, but I think that if I can solve theological problems in my mind, life will somehow make sense and all will be right with the world. Your one thing may be very different than mine. But we all have them.

It feels good to have a sense of mastery over something, to feel accomplished. It feels even better when we can get recognition from others for those accomplishments. Unfortunately, this satisfaction of mastery often clashes with reality when it comes to Christian discipleship. What can any of us really claim mastery over in things spiritual? In Jesus's day, there were folks that thought they really had their spiritual devotion buttoned up, that they had mastered it. The Rich Young Man is one who comes to mind.

Admiring the Rich Men

The Rich Young Man had the need to succeed. He wanted to know he was on the right track and doing what he needed to do to progress in life. This guy had it all. Observe,

> And behold, a man came up to him, saying, "Teacher, what good deed must I do to have eternal life?" And he said to him, "Why do you ask me about what is good? There is only one who is good. If you would enter life, keep the commandments." He said to him, "Which ones?" And Jesus said, "You shall not murder, You shall not commit adultery, You shall not steal, You shall not bear false witness, Honor your father and mother, and, You shall love your neighbor as yourself." The young man said to him, "All these I have kept. What do I still lack?" Jesus said to him, "If you would be perfect, go, sell what you possess and give to the poor, and you will have treasure in heaven; and come, follow me." When the young man heard this he went away sorrowful, for he had great possessions. (Matthew 19:16–22)

Let me make a few observations about this short exchange. This guy, the Rich Young Man, and the Pharisees often become scapegoats. It's obvious that they are smug, self-righteous, and holier-than-thou. But we are so familiar with many Bible narratives that we forget they apply to us. At least I do. "Surely, I'm not like an uptight Pharisee" or "Boy, the Rich Young Man sure missed Jesus's point." From the outside looking in, I can see how clueless some of these characters are, but I fail to see how often my own life mirrors these characters.

First, let's look at the identity of the Rich Young Man. The description from the passage itself is a dead giveaway. Depending on the Bible translation you read, the header for the section either reads "The Rich Young Man" (ESV and RSV), or "Rich Young Ruler" (NASB and NKJV). While the

headers in our Bibles were inserted into the text after translation, I'll use "Rich Young Ruler" because, well, it'll be more
fun that way. For better or worse, at least in our day and
age, the young and the rich rule social media and take up
the majority of pop culture's bandwidth. Music performers,
actors and actresses, and young, prodigy tech entrepreneurs
don the covers of magazines at the grocery store checkout
aisle. Many of us hang on their 140 character quips of wisdom
through social media where connection to the young, hip,
influential, and wealthy becomes a sort of vicarious fountain
of youth.

The cultural landscape of the Rich Young Ruler's day is
worlds apart from our own, and we don't know the backstory
of this guy's life. For our purposes, let's assume a story from
the perspective of our twenty-first-century experience. Let's
name this rich, young man Chet.

Chet always showed promise. Even from a young age his
mom knew he was something special. He was putting square
pegs into square holes way before the other little tykes in pre-
school. He was always on top with straight As from kindergar-
ten through university. He was on the honor roll every year,
and he was a letterman in school sports, including baseball and
football. He was voted most likely to succeed in his high school
yearbook. He was in clubs and committees that actually made
a difference around the schools he attended and the communities he lived in. There he was with impeccable presidential-like
hair and a smile, dressed in a casual, khaki-colored suit (it was
the 1980s).

Chet was the kind of guy we love to hate. In actuality, he
was a decent dude. He didn't only hang out with the jocks and
the pretty girls; he was nice to everybody. He hung out with
the band geeks, Mathletes, and stoners alike.

A few years later he was the darling of the law school he
attended. He graduated with high honors as the valedictorian
—gave the graduation speech and everything. Since graduation he's been putting bad guys behind bars. He has all the

accoutrements of success too: a BMW (although, unlike most fine German sports car drivers, he's actually a considerate driver), a mansion perched up on a hill (in a gated community), a wife who perfectly balances social and civic life in the community, and three kids who score straight As. But wouldn't you know it, you still can't hate the guy because he's legitimately nice and caring. He volunteers down at the soup kitchen on a regular basis too. Face it, Chet is an all-around good guy. He has it all. Most people covet his life, and yet he needs to ensure he's crossed every "t" and dotted every "i". He's been moral. Pious. Caring. Generous. But he has to be sure he's done all that is expected of him.

THE "ONE THING" NEEDED FOR SPIRITUAL SUCCESS

One day Chet comes to Jesus and says, "Hey, good teacher, I've done pretty well for myself in life. I'm feeling blessed. I've worked hard, tried my best to do what's right and give back to the community. But, you know, Jesus, I just need to make sure I've done everything as thoroughly as I should. What's the one thing I need to do to have eternal life?"

Have you ever asked what "one thing" you can do to make over your life? For me, this is related to knowledge. When an idea embeds into my brain, I scour every resource I can on the subject and devour it. I crave information because, for me, information unlocks the door of understanding, understanding is mastery, and mastery is freedom. Is that weird? You have your own version of this lively pursuit. You and I are not so different from the Rich Young Ruler. We're all looking for mastery of some sort.

According to the text, the Rich Young Ruler had done pretty well at mastery. He'd obeyed the commandments as a matter of course ever since he was a child. That's more than most of us can say. But while many of us can't claim this kind perfection, maybe we'd settle for just "one thing" to master. We live in a sea of three-simple-steps-to-a-successful-life programs.

Books that claim you can conduct a thriving business in four hours a week. One thing that you can do to declutter and get your life back. The one daily exercise that will deliver six-pack abs. What each of these "one things" promises is that you'll get your life back. It will make things easy, less stressful. The "one thing" promises success, happiness, and contentment in relationships. And yet, although people keep reading (and writing) these books, the problems are never really solved. Instead it seems to me that depression is on the rise, that people are more stressed and less sure of their place in the world than ever before. So much for that "one thing" fixing our lives.

"One Thing" Example #1: The Quiet Time

How many of us have confessed to churchgoing friends or to a Christian leader that our spiritual life feels dry or that we consistently "struggle" with that same-old besetting sin, and we're asked the boilerplate question: "Well, have you been in the Word much lately? Do you have a regular quiet time?" The quiet time seems to have become the answer to all our spiritual ails.

The image of a "quiet time" is almost fetishized. Now, thanks to social media, many of us have seen people broadcast their devotional time to the world. A picture of their Bible, a cup of coffee, and a few highlighters sprawled on the table. In fact, the whole idea has been parodied in a spoof you can find online that made the rounds in 2014 called "Christian Girl Instagram," a fictitious commercial advertising a fictitious book about how to capture a great photo to immortalize and broadcast to the world your cozy morning time with God. What makes this video funny is that it highlights something those of us in the Christian community are well aware of already—that many Christians consider a "quiet time" the cure-all for all spiritual disease or a daily Christian engine tune-up that we can't possibly live without.

Or maybe it's funny because those who make it a practice to lay out their Bible, perfectly prepared latte, and an array of highlighters to capture a stylized photo need to justify to the social media-watching world that their spiritual priorities in life are straight. But those of us who get a laugh out of this shouldn't feel so smug. We have our self-justifying blind spots too.

"One Thing" Example #2: Attend a Revival Event

Then there are the big Christian events. It could be summer camp or an on-the-road crusade that comes to town. There's a kind of afterglow to these events. We feel encouraged in our faith, strengthened, and given a new sense of resolve. Much like the results of a good motivational talk, special Christian events often put wind in our sails and provide space to get back on track spiritually and get "recommitted to the Lord"—for a while anyway.

As a fairly new Christian in the late 1980s, I attended a Power Team event. The mere mention of this undoubtedly causes chuckles among readers between the ages of about 35 and 50. The Power Team was a troop of strongmen, bodybuilders, and athletes that traveled the country speaking at schools about the dangers of drugs, the benefits of self-esteem, and social responsibility. At these talks they would make an invitation to a bigger event at a local church—or in their heyday, an arena—and pull out all the stops.

They would rip phone books in half, blow up hot-water bottles until they exploded, break out of handcuffs, and karate chop stacks of bricks in half—all of it as a way to illustrate what one can achieve when filled with the power of God. This may seem hokey now, but remember that this was the heyday of Arnold Schwarzenegger and Jean-Claude Van Damme movies, American Gladiator, and monster truck rallies.[1] Coupling the manly-man image with Christianity was a welcomed idea because some equated the average Christian man with an image of a pencil-necked, wimpy, Ned Flanders type of dork.

As a sixteen-year-old guy, I went to one of these arena events. If I'm remembering correctly, I thought the whole show was a little silly. But I belonged to a new tribe of people, and these were the kinds of things they did. They attended boisterous strongman arena shows and talked about God. I was a part of the youth group, and this is what they did. I thought I could learn to like it. Again, some of us love exciting Christian events and catching the next "move of the Spirit." These events help us to feel a part of a cutting edge. They help keep us energized when the rest of life is ho-hum. And if we can achieve that "one thing" of regularly feeling the excitement of spiritual fireworks, then we can ensure we're on the forefront of what God is doing in the world.

"One Thing" Example #3: The Unlocking Your Destiny Tape Series

Around the same time (as in the second example), there was a tape series that made the rounds as a "must-listen." The series was about the key to unlocking your God-given destiny. A mentor of mine felt it was important that I listen to the series, and he lent me the tapes (yes, cassette tapes!). I remember it clearly: that stupid tape set sat there, un-listened to, silently judging me. They were supposed to unlock my destiny. Instead they attracted dust. Though the phrase "find your destiny" wasn't a regular part of my sixteen-year-old vocabulary, the idea was important to me. According to my mother, I was very concerned about my future career as early as junior high. It should come as no surprise that I never listened to the finding-your-spiritual-destiny tape series, and after a few months it was time to return the tapes. I felt really guilty about not listening to them—not only guilty, but anxious. Maybe I had passed by the "one thing" I needed to know about unlocking my God-given destiny. The "one thing" needed to unlock my destiny to make sense of my sixteen-year-old world (and the rest of my future for that matter) would have taken a measly couple hours of listening to a transformative tape series. That's all the investment it would have taken. But the moment slipped me by, and I feared that maybe I'd never truly know God's will for my life.

Whether we're looking for career advice, tips for healthy living, or principles for a deeper, more devoted and heartfelt faith, we all have fallen for these "one thing" activities or experiences. I beat my head against the wall chasing after reading one-year Bible devotions, attending a revival event, listening to all the anointed teachers who could help me unlock my destiny, and devouring a stack of books. Just like the Rich Young Ruler who needed to ensure his spiritual life was all it could be, we need to feel as though we're doing something good for ourselves—that we're progressing and maturing. See, we're not that different from the Rich Young Ruler after all. How about you? What's your one thing?

WINNING THE CHECKLIST

Let's look back at Jesus's short exchange with the Rich Young Ruler again.

> And behold, a man came up to him, saying, "Teacher, what good deed must I do to have eternal life?" And he said to him, "Why do you ask me about what is good? There is only one who is good. If you would enter life, keep the commandments." He said to him, "Which ones?" And Jesus said, "You shall not murder, You shall not commit adultery, You shall not steal, You shall not bear false witness, Honor your father and mother, and, You shall love your neighbor as yourself." (Matthew 19:16–19)

The young man asked Jesus the path to eternal life. Jesus's response seems almost parochial: love God and love your neighbor, keep all the Ten Commandments. The Rich Young Ruler was looking for that leg up on all the mundane commandments business, a key to the higher life. Jesus's initial response must have been disappointing to the young man. Essentially, Jesus said do all the stuff you say you've already been doing. The Rich Young Ruler was looking to climb up to spiritual success. Jesus might as well have crumpled up his checklist and thrown it into the trash.

Though we can't know with complete accuracy this man's inner thoughts or intentions, he went away deflated, unable to obey Jesus's commands. Until then he'd found his way upstream and was enjoying a prestigious career as some sort of ruler. Maybe he'd hoped that Jesus would give him another checklist he could succeed with, climb up with and attain. What happens next is a surprise.

THE KINDNESS OF BACK-BREAKER JESUS

Though I quoted the passage from Matthew 19 above, I really like the commentary the Gospel of Mark adds after the Rich Young Ruler responds with, "I've kept all the religious rules since I was a kid." Mark 10:21 says, "And Jesus, looking at him, *loved* him . . ." (italics mine). Get that? Jesus loved him. Guess what Jesus does next? He loves the Rich Young Ruler by breaking his back with the weight of an impossible task: sell all you have and give it all to the poor and follow me.

"You know what, Chet? There is one thing that you lack. How about you sell the house, the BMW, and your Jet Ski? You go into the office tomorrow, quit the firm, and sell off your portion of the partnership. Once the check clears, you go and disperse all that money to the poor. Go to the gospel mission—you know the one in the seedy part of downtown— cut them a big fat check. You're an upstanding guy, so I know you can do it. After that, come right back here and follow me. One thing though—I'm homeless. Well, actually I sleep under the interstate bridge down in the valley. And crowds of needy people are always hounding me, and I don't always have time to eat . . ."

Poor Chet! That was a price he didn't expect to pay. Chet had worked hard in life in order to always be on top. The list Jesus gave him in his second response was utterly undoable because it didn't involve Chet winning, but him losing. So Chet went away sad.

Some believe that Jesus was delivering a prescriptive word to all believers—that all believers should be more committed to the poor and live simply so that others may simply live. There's something good to be gleaned from that idea. However, I think Jesus was doing something more profound here.

Rather than being a prescriptive text, this is a descriptive text based on what Jesus knew the Rich Young Ruler needed in the moment. Jesus set the bar so high that there was no place to go but down. Jesus set the Rich Young Ruler free to lose for once in his life. He'd been living a life based on winning and achieving up to that point. Imagine if Jesus had just given him a religious chore list. He would have checked all those items off the list, perhaps feel self-justified in his achievement, and trudged back to Jesus for another morale boost. The Rich Young Ruler expected to get a checklist in order to win at what he perceived he was already winning at! Jesus was preparing the Rich Young Ruler for something good that, unfortunately, he didn't seem to stick around to hear.

THE ONE THING = NOTHING

Jesus calls us to a life of radical commitment and obedience to him, no doubt. And if we're honest with ourselves, we know we're not living up to the demand; to be a disciple is to live within that tension. If we were living up to those high demands, we wouldn't need Jesus. The one thing we truly lack in the Christian life is—nothing.

A few verses later, Jesus addresses the disciples, "'Children, how difficult it is to enter the kingdom of God! It is easier for a camel to go through the eye of a needle than for a rich person to enter the kingdom of God.' And they were exceedingly astonished, and said to him, 'Then who can be saved?'" (Mark 10:24–26). Jesus's disciples were a bunch of working class, ragtag jokers. A well-educated, culturally savvy, and influential person with money would have come in handy. The Rich Young Ruler would have been a welcomed addition to the posse. Yet Jesus says getting Chet into heaven is like getting a camel through the eye of a needle. Translation: it's impossible. Fortunately, this isn't the end of the scene.

"Jesus looked at them and said, 'With man this is impossible, but with God all things are possible'" (Matthew 19:26). The Rich Young Ruler couldn't bring anything with him into that exchange with Jesus. Not his wealth, his title as a ruler, or his moral report card. What he didn't have was nothing. When we go looking to accomplish that one thing in our lives that we believe will make life complete, we are unknowingly on a path of self-justification. I'm convinced that there is something deeply ingrained in human beings that seeks self-justification. Even beyond the solid-gold theological reality of justification, whether you are a believing person or not, we all feel a deep-seated need to be told, or at least to believe within ourselves, that somehow we're OK. We want to know that, despite our flaws, in the end our failings aren't the last word about who we are.

Consider my botched testimony scene from earlier in the chapter. The one thing I was after was knowledge. I needed others to perceive me as a knowledgeable person. Why? It's embarrassing to admit, but it's because I want people to think I'm smart so they will like me. The one thing I didn't have in that moment was nothing.

This nothing is something Jesus can work with. There's no moral transaction from you that needs to take place in order for Jesus to draw near. No trophy on the shelf, no stack of egghead books to consume, no fat paycheck to earn, no academic credentials to achieve, not even an act of social justice performed. Jesus takes you and me just as we are. He takes the scabs, bruises, the 2 a.m. indiscretions, and all. Fortunately for you and me, God loves and accepts us despite our self-justifying behaviors. In that moment of self-justification in front of the church all those years ago, I couldn't have been any more loved by God than I already was and am. To know that I am always unconditionally loved carries with it a great sense of relief. The pressure's off.

Chapter 3
Movement Leader Jesus

Ten years ago we were among the thousands of irrationally optimistic Americans who bought a house they couldn't afford.[1] The specifics of the loan were a mess, and it was a straight-up bad idea. No excuses. The housing economy was booming at the time so we sold our previous house. We made a good profit from the sale and bought another house in a nicer neighborhood with expansive living room space.

I'm rarely lured into the idea that bigger, newer, or slicker is better. Sports car commercials seem silly to me. Given the choice, I'd drive a beater, dented old pickup over a clean new car. Whenever I see a newly constructed home in my neighborhood, it looks ugly and out of place. To the chagrin of my wife, I still wear certain twenty-year-old clothing items. (Let it be known this wardrobe sloth means I am in possession of the world's most comfortable threadbare T-shirt known to mankind.) But our home purchase was an exception—and it was a doozy.

Big Home = Big Mission

At the time, our church community was all about being "on mission." Today that phrase makes me gag a little bit. The saying within the church community went, "don't be a consumer of the culture, but invest in the community and plant roots." This "investing" motto included committing to purchasing a home as well as doing other things. As we planted roots in our community, we strove to live for the greater good of our neighborhood.

During this time my wife and I were leaders of a thriving home group. But the growth presented a practical problem. There was nowhere left for our friends to sit. Why undergo the pains of splintering off into another group? We'd just get a house with a bigger living room. I'm only half joking. Conveniently, there was a larger house for sale just down the street. It had a nice big price tag too. But, you know, we believed God would bless it, and he'd figure out a way to make it work. We just had to walk in faith and everything would turn out somehow. After all, growing a home group is the spiritual, "on mission," and faithful thing to do.

Lots of factors informed our buying a larger home. Wrongheaded ideas abounded—like using numerical growth as a barometer of spiritual significance. The culture within our church confirmed this idea. Good old-fashioned capitalism punctuated by the real estate boom flattered us. Were we a part of a movement of God or had consumerism tickled our ears? I'm not sure anymore.

The Insulating Effects of "Mission" Amidst Real Life

Watching our home group and church grow was exciting. But in hindsight, that growth was not sustainable. Our church had swallowed the cultural myth that growth was a virtue in and of itself. The demands to commit to more volunteerism mounted. After many years of this, we found ourselves within a church bubble. The result was the church became more and more insular. Ironically, all the spiritual busywork left us with no margin for much of a life outside the church. So much for mission.

And yet, many of us can relate to the desire to be a part of a quick-changing movement full of excitement. In such movements there's often growth in church attendance and a charismatic leader at the helm. Some people come to trust in

Jesus for the first time. It was especially exciting for us as long-time believers to experience renewed faith. To be included in such a thing makes us feel significant; it certainly made *us* feel significant. But day-to-day life is not always so exciting. As it turns out the Christian faith is more lawn mowing, bill paying, washing dishes, and tending to difficult relationships than Excitement Church 3000. We'd prefer a light show and fog machine, but the small things are the very guts of the gospel parables. Jesus often spoke of little, inconsequential things.

Christian life on the ground centers on plain church rhythms prescribed in the Great Commission. It's regular, by-the-book preaching, teaching, and starting new churches to do the same. But when the invisible, humble presence of the kingdom becomes rote and boring, we get restless. Then we go looking for something flashy, shiny, and new. We chase reports of spiritual fireworks.

Chasing Spiritual Fireworks

Twenty years ago I knew people who traveled to a revival event that reportedly took place in a Vineyard church near the Toronto airport. What was deemed a "move of the Spirit" in truth turned out to be religiously themed temporary group insanity. People were barking like dogs, falling into fits of uncontrollable laughter, and there were experiences of spiritual drunkenness all in the name of Jesus. But let's not be too judge-y here.

We all get caught up in our own brand of hype, don't we? We tune into influential preachers with large followings and larger egos. We are drawn to movement leaders keen to pop culture who know how to draw in large crowds of mostly young people. Eventually, discontentment sets in and we're tempted to think to ourselves, "If we just had the right kind of church facility, a charismatic leader, and a rocking praise band, God would bless our efforts, the church would grow, and we'd have more influence in our communities." In short, we become discontent that we'll miss out on something big. We start thinking we'll miss the next move of the Spirit. I've experienced this discontent firsthand.

Humble Beginnings at the Neighborhood Pentecostal Church

As a new convert, I began attending a small Pentecostal church on the edge of town. I felt a little awkward in this church as one of only four or five teenagers and definitely the only punk rocker. I used to get the stink-eye from old ladies on a pretty regular basis. When my buddy and I first visited the youth group, the leader told us something unforgettable (although I'm sure he was well-intentioned). He said, "I'm just going to be honest, guys. When you came in the room, I felt the strong presence of Satan. Out of curiosity, do those chains on your boots represent your spiritual bondage?" True story, but I'll save those tales for another time—and therapy.

Somehow, by God's miraculous intervention, I was able to overlook the offense—or at least I overlooked the offense enough to continue attending the church. But I did drop youth group like it was hot. I had never read the Bible before, and I couldn't get enough. I went to church every Sunday and attended every prayer meeting I could. I was learning the baby steps of the Christian faith.

The memories that stand out most these twenty-some years later are the experiences. Church was as exciting as a rodeo. And on the chance you could get a seat closer to the pastor, you'd be more likely to catch a case of the Holy Ghost Goose Bumps. That was kind of a joke at the time, but only sort of.

Word of Faith TV preachers of the day were popular among this congregation. Preachers like Benny Hinn, who is a traveling evangelist with a comb-over hairstyle, white suit, and sweaty brow. He claimed the gift of healing and had particular trademarks. During his speeches he'd get the "Holy Ghost fever" and a near riot among observers would ensue.

Somehow, the louder and sweatier he got, the more people hit the ground. For some reason, the Holy Spirit likes to knock people off their feet. How that experience is spiritually edifying, I'm not sure. But as a newish believer, I rooted for these preachers. I willingly attended similar events and would even stay up late watching these preachers on TV. I wanted to do the will of God, after all. I feared if I didn't have a front-row seat to how the Holy Spirit was messing up everybody's hair, I'd miss out in life and God's movement, big time. When things appear fun, interesting, and exciting and we miss the party invitation, a fear of missing out sets in. Been on Facebook lately?

Church Hopping Fueled by Fear of Missing Out

If there were any cultural environment for the fear of missing out to be best cultivated, it would be the twenty-first century. Social media is at our hip pocket twenty-four seven, and our tendency toward voyeurism is easily piqued. Mostly, this only causes envy. It seems as if everyone else's life is so much more alluring and accomplished than our own. Somebody out there is maximizing their fun quotient in the out of doors and getting a suntan while you're stuck on the couch getting pastier by the second and sulking late at night in the glow of your Facebook feed. See, look. All those happy, beautiful, interesting people are interacting with other dynamic funny people. They read provocative, mind-expanding books. They enjoy their perfect families in the most picturesque settings. All while eating food worthy of studio photography three times each day.[2]

If you follow churches that are tech savvy, then Fear of Missing Out (FOMO) has undoubtedly edged its way into your spiritual imagination too. Somewhere across the country in a cool urban area there's an exciting ministry that gets it; a place where dozens are baptized every week. They're able to prove it through amazingly heartfelt photography posted to their social media feed. They show photos of the newly baptized, post-dunk, dripping wet, both fists pumping the sky in Jesus-saves victory.

Those same churches always seem to have the most rocking-est bands. And they play music that would fit on the radio. Even their hymn renditions don't sound weird or cheesy to your friends. The pastor? He's like a stand-up comedian! But it's not just shallow entertainment. No, he preaches the Word. And it's convicting. He quotes current movies and song lyrics from trendy bands. He addresses hot-button cultural issues head-on. He's unflinching in telling truth. On top of it all, the church is growing like crazy. And you know it because you're subscribed to the email newsletter and get all the weekly stats.

It'd be so great to be part of a move of God like that, wouldn't it? Instead, you're stuck in a church in Podunk, Iowa, that still sports orange carpet from the 1970s. Your pastor just quoted a REO Speedwagon song lyric in last Sunday's sermon. And the old ladies in the front row get a little agitated when the praise band drummer hits the skins too hard. If only the congregation and the pastor would get a clue. "C'mon, people! Update the programming! Speak about relevant topics from the pulpit! Maybe then we'd reach our community just like that awesome trendy church does."

This is how it goes—this discontent with "uncool" church, the fear of missing out on the next big move of the Spirit. I've lived this. I jumped ship from church to church as a new Christian, not because of theological conviction, but because I wanted a "cooler" church experience.

Back to my experience with the little Pentecostal church. Church was in no way dull. The congregation got plenty sweaty during the praise service, and the pastor yelled during sermons on a pretty regular basis. But there was a pretty major cultural disconnect eating at me, and I could tell an inevitable change was on the horizon. The average age of the congregation was about sixty-three—all fans of both kinds of music: Country *and* Western. During the praise services, a few other rebels and I had taken to clapping on the upbeat—the two and four count—to spice things up a bit. This rebellion resulted in coordination confusion for about 50 percent of the congregation. We started to get the stink-eye from the praise leader and the situation worsened. One morning in a peevish, pursed-lipped, matronly tone she made a sober announcement. Between songs, she shared that the Lord desired for us to be unified and of one accord. Her eyes widened to punctuate the words "one accord." It was like hate-lasers beamed out of her eyes in our direction. Message received. The church would resume clapping to the downbeat, whitebread-ness restored. My time to move on had come.

Church Hop 1: The Band Was Way Better

This decision to move on to a new church was peppered with other factors too. For one, I was suspicious of the whole signs and wonders racket. Maybe I wasn't in step with the Spirit, but the whole falling over when "God showed up" was a little much for me. It was weird. In addition to my suspicions, I was lugging around the thousand-pound iron ore guilt of an unhealthy relationship. All this in the context of a church that was so bent on holiness that even listening to Christian rock was suspect. Because, you know, drumbeats are wrought in the fires of hell. Country-Western Pentecostalville had become a drag. The perfect guilt and shame cocktail triggered in me the need to hide. So I left to go attend a bigger church where the music was better and I could get lost in the midst of the people.

The band I played drums in at the time started picking up more gigs, and I was meeting other like-minded musicians, many of whom attended a Calvary Chapel in the city, so I started attending there myself. At Calvary, artistic expression was encouraged. Imagine that. Calvary Chapel churches began in the 1970s as a sort of haven for young hippies. So there was not just toleration, but a full-on embrace of those who identified with the counterculture. I fit right in. And the adults in leadership didn't doubt my faith because of my safety-orange dyed hair either. I know—shallow, right? But c'mon, I was nineteen years old. I didn't have to miss out anymore and I had found my new church home. Well, maybe.

Though I associated with this crowd, I kept my involvement at arm's length. Several friends got involved as mentors in youth ministry and went on mission trips. Every so often I attended the college ministry on Wednesday nights. Every few months I'd go to church on Sunday mornings.

Fast-forward about five years. With the shame-anchor still in tow due in large part to another failed one-year relationship that ended ugly and in plain sight of my church community and the newness of welcomed artistic expression worn off, I'd pretty well fallen out of church community. I stopped attending church altogether for about a year.

Church Hop 2: The Congregation Was Smarter

Then, when I wasn't looking for it at all, I read about a new church plant and—ta-da!—fear of missing out rose up in me again. See, at Calvary both beer and end-times theory were big deals. Beer consumption was thought of as bad. To me, it seemed like a happy Christian duty. Accepting church-approved end-times theory was important. To me, it was not. Embracing weirdo creatives like me required creativity . . . and then sneaking lots of Jesus into the message. And if you didn't agree with this evangelistic approach, your creative motives became suspect. I was feeling burnt out by it all.

Then along came this cool new church plant. The mission statement referenced smart, challenging books I'd read. They valued the arts and reaching out to the music community without the propagandistic approach to evangelism. They weren't legalistic about drinking alcohol. And they didn't seem too concerned about having an ironclad theory about the end times all mapped out. I was sold.

I started attending this new church plant, and it was exciting. People who were either de-churched or un-churched fit right in. The theological foundation was old-school evangelical, but the expression of the worship service was all our own. It was exciting, and for the first time in my life, I got involved in church volunteerism. My life began to change for the better. I met my wife there. We started a family, and we were in it for the long haul as "lifers." We were members there for seventeen years. We saw the church grow from a small gathering to over ten thousand. It ended up being a pretty big deal in the evangelical community. But sadly, it all came crashing down just shy of the twenty-year mark once bad leadership practices started catching up.[3]

I wouldn't say attending three different churches over a ten-year period constitutes serial church hopping. But my impulses for switching were always to go after something new and relevant, something more cutting edge. I don't think it was wrong to change gears and worship in new places. In fact, as my theology has developed over the years, changing lanes was inevitable. Despite the theological disparities, each church introduced people to Jesus faithfully, I think. The churches weren't entirely the problem. The problem was also me. I wanted to be connected to something "important," something that had credibility in some way. I wanted to be part of a church that reflected a sophisticated Christianity that I could be proud of and show off to my unbelieving friends. I wanted a version of Christianity that wasn't . . . embarrassing. I wanted to be attached to a movement or a leader that was doing something impactful, and I've noticed this fear of missing out in those around me as well. Here's an example of what I mean.

Our Church Wish Lists

Recently I met a friend for coffee who was experiencing the difficulty of finding a new church. He had been a part of the large church I just mentioned. He'd moved out of town for a year to pursue business, and found another church out east with similar programming: great production; an engaging, funny, and gifted preacher; and an entertaining children's ministry that their kids loved. When he moved back to our area, he found our home church had disintegrated and shut its doors. As we sat sipping our coffee, he described the kind of church he longed for again: one where the church facility was nice and had ample parking and where the children's ministry was fun for the kids. But the big-ticket item on his wish list was that the church had to be led by an entertaining and dynamic pastor. He wanted to be at a church where he felt like he was part of an exciting move of the Spirit. He wanted to be a part of the kind of place he'd become accustomed to.

I don't blame him. The entire wish list he outlined makes complete sense to me. I'd rather be in a pleasing space with good music and pleasant aesthetics on a Sunday morning. I'd rather listen to a message spoken with personality than get lulled to sleep by a monotone delivery. And yet, aside from the wish list, there was an undercurrent to our conversation. He didn't like the idea of not belonging to an exciting movement of God. What he'd experienced at his old church felt vital. But of all the churches he visited, he couldn't quite find that same exciting quality.

Over the next year, I heard similar complaints from others who were exiled from the community because our church had shut down. There was a general feeling of displacement due to not having a home within the extraordinary. It was like a popular kid who moves to a new town and assumes their innate specialness, but then realizes they have to start over again at a new high school and elbow their way into a new caste system.

The Flattery of Church Success Envy

Years ago, before I became a volunteer pastor, I attended a Christian leader's conference. This was the first year of what is now a well-known annual conference. While attending this conference, I realized for the first time that others viewed my church trailblazing a movement. I was caught off guard.

One afternoon I attended a meet-and-greet lunch with a group of folks in ministry. One of the pastors I served with pointed me out and made a genuine and kind comment about me—something about how I'd been serving in the church's music ministry. A few in attendance took note of my church association, and for the rest of the conference, I felt like a mini-celebrity. I soon realized my church association lent me credibility. I had the attention of a group of people who might not have been interested in what I had to say otherwise. This was the first time it occurred to me that church success envy was a real thing. Between conference sessions, some of us gathered at a pub, and a small crowd fired questions at me to better understand the secret to the success of our ministry. How could they put the best practices in place so their churches could grow in size and influence as ours had? For maybe the first time, people doing important things wanted to ask me questions. And I wasn't even ordained yet. It was flattering, and I felt proud. That day I knew I was a part of something way bigger than me, and bigger even than our local growing church. A small group of people had heard me out, and I felt empowered to make a difference. To be honest, it was kind of intoxicating.

All That Glitters Is Not Gold

In all my movement-chasing pit stops, the common theme is grasping after the attractive and glitzy. As much as I hate to admit it, appearances mattered to me. This is the default of the human heart, isn't it? I'd heard things like "living things grow" (ironically, mold and cancer grow too), or "a healthy church is a growing church." A ministry's efforts to hold the attention of a generation not known for church attendance must be a move of the Spirit, right? Well, the rocking praise band and the jokey pastor might have had something to do with it too.

To be a part of something cutting edge, exciting, and important makes *us* feel important. I thought I'd get more satisfaction in belonging to each exciting, new movement. But each movement, each new church, failed to provide that satisfaction. The novelty always wore off, or the leaders bombed and the doors were shut for good. The thing that seemed to promise belonging and fulfillment turned to alienation.

GOD'S PRESENCE DOES NOT REQUIRE A LIGHT SHOW (HE SHOWS UP IN BREAD AND WINE)

There's a reason you're reading this book. Maybe you've gone through the ministry ringer or you're tempted to scramble after the glitz too. You may feel unsatisfied in your own church, but hold off on running after the next movement. Ask yourself a few questions first: Is the gospel preached? Is the message the good news of Jesus dying and rising for sinners like you and me? Are people getting baptized, and does the pastor get bread and wine into your mouth? If so, then you have yourself a church, and the Spirit is present. If you can add to that list a congregation that is relationally warm and isn't shocked when you're a jerk, you've hit the jackpot. The apostle Paul reminds us in Romans 10 that we don't have to ascend to the heavens or go to the depths in order to get Jesus. He is present when his words are spoken. Do you get that? If your dorky, culture-stunted pastor still stuck on 1980s soft rock is preaching the words of Jesus to you, then God is with you. You don't need a light show, a sweaty, dynamic preacher, or a radio hit praise band. You need to hear about sin and grace, see some people get wet, and taste the bread and wine.

I'm reminded of this every Sunday. The church I now attend is much smaller. The services are quieter. The praise song arrangements are simple, and there aren't any stage lights. The sermons are good. And you know what? I get Jesus. Every Sunday I get Jesus. When I take the bread in my hand, dip it in the cup, and feel that excess wine dribble onto my hand, I know Jesus has given his body and blood for me. He feeds me with himself. Sometimes I wonder why God used bread and wine to deliver grace to us. But then I think, *maybe it's because when we're eating it's the only time we shut up and stop talking.* We stop talking about our future plans or even our own failures. While our mouths are busy consuming, God gives us the pure gift of himself. You don't have to do anything special or be anywhere special in order to receive that.

If you're feeling like a chump for being overly impressed by cool church or a narcissistic leader that built the ministry on you and your friends' backs and then disregarded you when you got "off mission" by asking questions, if you're feeling a little shallow about falling for church discontent or fear of missing out, you're in good company. Maybe you took the bait of Movement Leader Jesus, but you're realizing it was all hype and the "movement" lacks depth and substance. Turns out Movement Leader Jesus was full of hot air, and wasn't the real Jesus after all. Allowing yourself to feel the disappointment in a failing church community stings. As the saying goes, "Hope deferred makes the heart sick" (Proverbs 13:12). As painful as it is, we can be glad for the letdowns. It means that God isn't allowing lesser things to take his place. Instead, he is giving you himself.

Chapter 4
Visionary Jesus

About a year ago, I was out with a buddy (we'll call him John) enjoying conversation over beers. We were at the Sloop Tavern, a working-class, sailor's dive bar down by the Ballard Lochs where the tugboats come in and out of Puget Sound. The conversation was a little heavy, so naturally, the occasion required that we "Sloopersize" our beers. John and I had worked alongside each other in ministry at the church mentioned in the last chapter that had imploded. We were on different teams, but each of us had worked with talented and creative people. We both felt we'd contributed meaningful work to the church. But we'd both since left vocational ministry.

For context's sake, John had grown up in a cultish, coercive church. As if going through one horrible church experience as a teenager wasn't enough, he was offered more Kool-Aid as an adult at another megachurch. It was surprising that he managed to hang in there and continue in the faith. John had been out of vocational ministry a couple years and had gotten involved in a much smaller church. He said something between swigs of beer about the philosophy of Christian mission that was simple, but profound. I'll never forget it.

VISIONARY LEADERSHIP

First, John outlined the visionary leadership we both had become accustomed to at the church we worked at. In a corporate business model, the key leader defines the mission for an organization. For example, a visionary leader may define a five-year plan and "cast vision" for the corporation's future financial success and growth. In a corporate environment, this makes complete sense. The purpose of a for-profit organization is to grow and make more money year after year.

With the leader's goals well defined, they employ talent who values the corporation's mission and can achieve its goals. John had a summary experience of "visionary leadership" where he recalled a memorable staff meeting. The lead pastor gave a three-point talk to a group of associates. What were the three markers of effective church leadership? "Results, results, results!" No talk of servant leadership, shepherding, or the church as the family of God, just boardroom bullying. Perform or else.

Tragically, John's experience is not uncommon. When this model is present in the church, it puts the church staff and congregation in service to the leader who defines success. In this sort of environment, the church staff is obligated to sell the "brand" of the leader. The church congregant's identity is handed to them like workers in support of a ready-made mission in a box. There's obvious value to well-organized and effective leadership within the church. But ministry life simply clashes with business-minded objectives. The church is a family, people loving one another, not a corporation selling a product or workers whose primary job is to feed their leader's ego by meeting corporate objectives.

Leaders with special leadership qualities attract followers who are flattered to be led by them. As if they were chosen to match the specialness of their leader. As if those privileged enough to call an especially gifted person their pastor must also be special themselves. This can have toxic ramifications on the church culture because both the leader and the church community need one another's reassurance that they are set apart from the crowd. Remember my story from the conference in the last chapter? My pastor pointed me out in a small group, and I had the opportunity to field questions from a group impressed by my connection to a famous church and pastor. It was a win-win for everybody. Flattering dynamics[1] in communities make for a perfect symbiotic social-stew between pastor and congregants.

These leaders understand the importance of the community having a voice, and they gladly take on the task of *being* the voice on their behalf. These leaders understand the community's longing to belong and make a difference. And a community's connection to a charismatic leader that represents these things on a community's behalf is empowering. People trust a charismatic leader to speak on their behalf, especially when they feel and have felt marginalized. The charismatic leader is the glue that holds the community together for something bigger than themselves. And the leader points the way toward a future hope of what the community can and ought to be.[2]

GOD HATES VISIONARY DREAMING

Dietrich Bonhoeffer, the famous German churchman, had a scathing critique of "visionary dreaming." Says Bonhoeffer,

> God hates visionary dreaming; it makes the dreamer proud and pretentious. The man who fashions a visionary ideal of community demands that it be realized by God, by others, and by himself. He enters the community of Christians with his demands, sets up his own laws, and judges the brethren and God himself accordingly. He stands adamant, a living reproach to all others in the circle of the brethren. He acts as if he is the creator of the Christian community, as if his dream binds men together. When things do not go his way, he calls the effort a failure. When his ideal picture is destroyed, he sees the community going to smash. So he becomes, first an accuser of his brethren, then an accuser of God, and finally the despairing accuser of himself.[3]

The problem with a visionary leader's agenda is that people fail and sin. The visionary leader with goals of what the church should look like isn't facing reality. In the process, they fail to engage what is happening right in front of them; they fail to engage broken people who need a shepherd. The visionary leader runs the deadly risk of not loving their church as it exists in the present. Rather, they love a church of their imagination, a bigger and better church of the future. That's not love for a congregation. That's love of one's ego. At worst, it's narcissism.

When followers buy into a leader's visionary dreaming, they follow them into a minefield of mutual disappointment. The inevitable outcome is burnout for the congregant and frustration for the leader. It's only a matter of time before there's a misstep and the carnage starts flying (usually the congregation). There are even worse scenarios when a narcissist is at the helm. Unfortunately, this is more common than we'd like to think. A narcissistic shepherd is an oxymoron. By definition, a shepherd leads sheep toward food and sustenance. But a narcissistic leader can't imagine a world where they're not the hero. Over time, some in the community realize they have not been fed. Rather, they've been sheared and devoured by an imposter—a hireling shepherd[4] who benefits from the worship they receive from their congregants but has no care for those who cannot unquestionably fall in line with their visionary agenda.

Shepherd Leadership

Fortunately, my friend John had found a new church home where the pastor wasn't "casting a vision" to recruit workers. Instead the pastor was a servant setting the table to feed God's people a spiritual feast. His description brought me back to the encouraging word of the apostle Paul's heart for the pastor. According to Ephesians 4, God gifts the pastoral office to the church. Not so that the leader might take pride in building an organization they can boast in, but so that the church might be built up to spiritual health and equipped for day-to-day life. "And he gave the apostles, the prophets, the evangelists, the shepherds and teachers, to equip the saints for the work of ministry, for building up the body of Christ" (Ephesians 4:11–12).

Despite denominational traditions, every believer comes into the church with a predefined mission. But it's Christ's mission, not the presumptuous plans of a "visionary leader." The church needs sound teaching and remembrance of all that our Lord has passed on to us. The church has already received the call to teach, serve communion, baptize, and evangelize; the church has been called to carry out the Great Commission. "And Jesus came and said to them, 'All authority in heaven and on earth has been given to me. Go therefore and make disciples of all nations, baptizing them in the name of the Father and of the Son and of the Holy Spirit, teaching them to observe all that I have commanded you. And behold, I am with you always, to the end of the age'" (Matthew 28:18–20).

Each person has a particular station and call on their life. This is more than mere jobs that we hold, but the vocation of our lives. By "vocation" I mean how God gets things done in the world through everyday, human efforts. He feeds us in part by gifting us with bakers who make bread that we eat. We're able to get around because someone tightened a screw with a torque wrench in a factory so the wheels on our cars don't fall off. Whether parent or child, leader or employee— we're called to love God with our whole hearts. We're called to love our neighbors as ourselves where God has placed us (Jesus's Great Commandment, Matthew 22:36–40).

With these passages in mind, it is clear that the pastor serves not as a visionary leader at the forefront of a movement, but in a vocation entrusted with particular duties. In faithful response to the Great Commission, a pastor's call is to spiritually nourish their congregants with the Word, to serve them God's gifts in the sacraments of communion and baptism, and to help them understand how to bless others in the station of life God calls them to (loving their neighbor).

My friend John's description of pastoral leadership and the remembrance of these Scriptures was much-needed balm to my soul. It was a conversational lifeline in a dark and depressing time. At the time, all I could see was a church functioning as a corporation, chewing good people up and spitting them out when they were no longer useful to the "mission."

The Chewed Up and Spit Out. The Beloved

At one time, my wife and I had a finger in four ministry pies simultaneously. And it kept us busy five nights a week. Keep in mind that I was not in "vocational ministry," but had a regular nine-to-five cubicle-tech job too. We didn't have little kids then so we had more time for our ministry endeavors. Still, being newly married and overcommitted was not good. I was in a type of training program to become a volunteer pastor (the training I mentioned in the last chapter). I was studying a lot, as well as working with a sponsoring pastor/friend who gave me specific ministry assignments. He had the good sense to tell me to scale back on my commitments so I could focus on a specific ministry instead of getting pulled in too many directions. That was a big help, and I'm thankful for the wisdom. But even after we scaled back, we were so committed to church programming that there was little margin for outside friendships or even the kind of evangelism the church encouraged in the first place. We were in a ministry bubble. Life was church; church was life.

If this sounds at all familiar, step back and ask yourself what the definition of "mission" is in your church. The Great Commission and the Great Commandment may theoretically be at the center of that definition. But often a subtle shift happens with ambitious leaders at the helm. Ambition, drive, and desire for growth in a church are good things, but ask yourself where this ambition comes from. If counting bodies in pews is a primary motivating factor beyond care of individual souls, it's time to be a redemptive pain in the ass and keep asking your leaders hard questions.

For those chewed up and spit out, burned out by such a church, remember this: you are God's beloved bride of Christ. God isn't asking you to join the cause to build a Christian soul-saving empire so that he'll love you. You are not a ministry worker bee needing to justify your existence with results. You are not just a body filling a pew counted in a spreadsheet. You are loved by Jesus Christ. Not the future-improved you or the worn-out—maybe even jaded—you. The present-tense you, just as you are.

Chapter 5
Pride and Despair

Nearly twenty years ago, on a bright, warm summer day, I was driving around with my mom running errands and mulling over a challenging theology book I had been reading. I had gotten hung up on a specific phrase and had been mulling it over all day. It read, "God's revelation has nothing whatever to do with morality."[1] There was something about the phrase that both bugged and intrigued me. I believed the author was right, but I didn't know why. That idea didn't quite sit right with my mom either, though our conversation continued and developed into a great talk about the meaning of grace. I don't think either of us had a grasp on what grace meant. In fact, I remember her asking me, "Can you explain what grace means?" I was at a loss for words and bumbled through a half-baked answer. I don't remember the conversation in its entirety now, but once we got on the topic of grace, it was pointed in the right direction.

Up until the moment of that exchange, I believed the common myth that the Bible is "the owner's manual for life" (or the just as popular "Basic Instructions Before Leaving Earth"). This idea puts the believer's morality skills in the spotlight and on center stage. If one can live according to this owner's manual, life is happy, personal achievements fall into place, and you'll leave a legacy and die happy. The problem is that this approach to life puts human beings in the driver's seat and makes God into a sort of cosmic butler as a means to our ends. (Think about that bumper sticker, "God is my co-pilot.") Or worse, it obligates God to pay us back for our winning efforts and wise living.

It's this line of thinking that characterizes the entire Life Coach Jesus enterprise so well. It's a playbook for life. Our false saviors exist only to help us achieve our own ends. Remember Brennan Manning's previous maxim from the introduction? "It is true that we make our images of God. It is even truer that our images of God make us." On top of this idol-flavored problem of ours, chumming around with Life Coach Jesus over a long period of time delivers a new set of problems nobody bargains for. And they're not good options. If you hang around Life Coach Jesus long enough, take it from me, you are cruisin' for a bruisin'. You're going one hundred miles per hour toward the wall of pride and despair, and things are about to get ugly.

In the wake of getting leveled by Life Coach Jesus, I realized I'd gone through a pretty robust period of pride. I thought I was living according to the owner's manual. I obeyed the playbook. But life had given me a pretty good lashing at that point, and I was in the throes of despair. I'd hit each wall and was beginning to feel bitter. My life options sucked. I didn't want to be a prideful creep by pretending I had the rule-keeping thing nailed down. But I also didn't want to have to crawl out of a pit of despair. At times it seemed like bailing from the whole program was the only option. I loved Jesus, but I wasn't, and seemingly could not, live up to the Christian program. I was in a lose-lose situation. But I didn't bail after getting smacked around by the life coach. I got back in the game with the movement leader and visionary periods of life as detailed in previous chapters. Then I got ground up in those gears too. And here I am, roughly twenty-five years later, a mangled mess and burnt out on church.

Let's take a step back and consider pride and despair in their native habitat. Maybe you'll be able to connect with where they have been evidenced in your own life.

PRIDEFUL RELIGIOSITY

Ah, the prideful religionist. Most of us have met this guy. The prideful religionist is an easy target to pick on. Just put a Pharisee hat and a synthetic, costume beard and bathrobe on 'em and you've got the perfect cardboard cutout to take aim at. Fictitious costumes aside, you know the type. The compliant Sunday-school overachiever who is sweaty handed and dry mouthed over the moral do's and don'ts. These folks buy into the idea that flawless spiritual discipline buys brownie points with God. These are the sort of folks who are uptight over loose living—alcohol and tobacco consuming, card playing, heavy metal listening and expletive dropping. They tend to have end-times theories perfectly charted out too.

But this stereotype is a little too easy to mock. As it turns out, there's a sort of pride that's not always easily detectable about this kind of person. Prideful Religionist Guy used to hide out in the small Pentecostal church I attended as a new Christian. He occasionally made guest appearances at the Calvary Chapel church a couple years later, but I did my best not to be exposed by him. I imagine Prideful Religionists wind up in every kind of church within Christendom.

The thing is, I was basically a mini Prideful Religionist guy when I attended the small Pentecostal church. That is, until I got a girlfriend. Then I went into hiding out of fear of being discovered as a sinning imposter. Then I skipped town to attend a different church to keep my secret.

PRIDEFUL RELIGION MAKES FOR GOOD NEIGHBORS

Spiritual pride doesn't always appear brazenly on the surface in an obvious, hateful Westboro Baptist, "God Hates All the Sinners" picket sign. Often those lugging spiritual pride around make great friends and neighbors. One professional man I was acquainted with comes to mind. He ran a successful business and had earned some educational kudos for himself. On the side, out of pure love and concern, he self-published books and gave motivational talks on the importance of personal Bible study. His care for people was authentic, and it was clear he was sacrificing time and commitment toward good endeavors. But then he said something that took me aback. He'd recently given one of his motivational talks encouraging Bible study. As he explained it, he passed around small slips of paper and had everyone anonymously write down how much time they'd spent in personal Bible study and dedicated prayer time in the last week. He made it clear that praying while taking a shower or driving didn't count. By personal Bible study he meant finding a quiet place with no distractions (preferably on your knees). Then he read over the slips and tallied the time. He compared the prayer time against other popular pastimes, like fiddling with electronic gadgets or looking at the TV. Then he graded the group on their abysmal performance. They spent an exponential amount of time gadget fiddling and TV viewing and very little, if any, time in personal devotions. He gave them an exhortation to adopt his Bible reading plan and stop being so spiritually lazy.

On the off chance anyone came away motivated to be better in "spiritual disciplines," it would have only come from a place of compulsion and guilt. There was a clear subtext in what he was sharing with me. He was nailing good devotional habits while his hearers clearly were not. Maybe I'm being too judge-y, but to me, the whole scenario smacked of spiritual pride. In the interest of fairness, no one is exempt from pride and I've had (and have) some nasty cases of it myself. I've already told the story of not being able to keep my hands off my girlfriend as a teenager and my simultaneous disdain for smoking, drinking, and listening to non-Christian music. Oh, the irony.

But maybe this pride policing is a little too easy. There are lots of other sorts of pride as well. It's easy to look back twenty-five years and spot our flaws. It's not so easy to see our pride in recent years, much less the present. However, for my part, I can say this: I spent sixteen-plus years in a community that made a really big deal of gender roles in the home. I still believe that the Bible has wisdom for how husbands and wives can best live together and how that might inform domestic life. But the fact is, I had a prideful mistrust for other believers who didn't see these issues eye to eye with me. I used to believe people with a different viewpoint on these issues weren't serious about their Bible reading. Men were created to lead the family and provide for them. Women were supposed to support their husbands and stay home with the kids. There was no wiggle room on the subject. Ahem . . . that's pride. Nowadays, I'm reconsidering my previously held views. Anymore, I get the willies whenever I hear people spouting this kind of stuff. I dunno, maybe I haven't parsed out all the original Greek words from Paul's Epistles adequately enough to have a strong position on the subject. I hope I'm growing in humility with those who have a different point of view.

Cultural Boundary Markers and Pride

I'm tempted to bash the preacher who championed this particular brand of gender roles pride. I'm pretty confident there's plenty to bash, but I'll leave that to professional bloggers. They're good at it. But he had followers (like me) for a reason. The congregation liked pride-filled messages because we were prideful ourselves.

Presently I'm struggling to make sense of what fueled this pride. On one hand, it was a tightfisted conviction within the community that what the Bible has to say about gender roles is normative in all times and places. But taking a hard stance on gender roles reflects fear. And perhaps fear is a flipside of pride. Templates for life provide safety and ready-made answers.

Answers are comforting. Not working within a narrow template feels too chaotic for some, and it creates uneasiness and fear. Throw into the mix general confusion regarding gender in society—what does it mean to be feminine, to be masculine—and fear is intensified. Then there are men who simply need to be in a position of power and control to feel OK about themselves. No doubt there were many factors at play, factors that will take time, thought, prayer, and a lot of repentance to work through.

At any rate, under this pride-filled and pride-inducing preaching, having our backsides handed to us was a regular occurrence. After a nice, concise gospel presentation, a strong prescription for what the new life looked like got tacked on to the end of the sermon on a regular basis. It was a one-dimensional script: "Now that you belong to Jesus, it's time to live a transformed life. Get married, have children (lots of them), buy a house, make lots of money, live up to traditional gender roles. Dads, be a hero to your wife and kids. Moms, stay home with the children and be a domestic acrobat with baked goods skills." Of course this is a summary. But it was a common theme. Over time this transformed life image metastasized as pride within our church community—myself included. Those who did not fit the narrow mold of this view of domestic life were suspect as slovenly Bible students and disobedient disciples.

Looking back, I see things differently. Our community had become so bent on secondary, non-salvation issues it was like Jesus stopped short of being our Savior. Instead, he'd become the champion of our own American Dream. I'd like to suggest that perhaps the incessant need within our community to make a mark on the world through a strongly prescribed, one-dimensional lifestyle was a problem.

It could be that many of our aspirations are only baptized worldly impulses meant to satiate our own self-focused desires. We strive for bigger, better, faster, shinier, and when pastors preach this, our hearts resonate—"yes, that's what I want too! He's such a dynamic leader who gets it!" This just

confirms what I said in the introduction about our latent theology of glory tendencies and our pride. There's a pretty good
chance God's goal isn't to gratify us with more. The life coach,
the spiritual checklist, the movement and visionary leader
promise big things, but in the end, they're false hopes with
an even bigger, fatter price tag. Maybe—just maybe—this is
what the Bible calls worldliness à la 1 John 2:16.[2] Truthfully, it's
spiritual jargon cloaking worldliness, a mere baptizing of the
desires of the flesh, the desire of the eyes, and the pride of life.

Developing an ear-tickling program based on a self-con-
gratulating American Dream is not hard. Who doesn't want to
make tons of money, raise compliant kids, and enjoy wedded
bliss—whether they're a believer in Jesus or not? Bookstores
are full of junk detailing three steps to a better life; even better
when the message includes a strong component of shame.
Many of us are bent on feeling bad about ourselves, and when
a charismatic personality compellingly points out the problem and solution, it's an easy sell. Tickling ears with a best-life
message is easy. Preaching and practicing non-judgmental,
no-strings-attached grace in a diverse community in different
stages of life and maturity . . . that's tough.

THE FLIP SIDE OF PRIDE: DESPAIR

As a little kid, I used to have horrible night terrors. It went on
for years. Fortunately, by the time I was a teenager, the nightmares subsided. But in my twenties it was replaced with a new
sleep experience that has always been tough to describe. As
I was slowly waking up, I'd find myself in a half-awake, half-
sleep state. I had an awareness that I was lying in my bed, and
sometimes I could hear the muffled, underwater-like sounds
of my roommate bumping around in the kitchen. It was like
the experience of lying in a 100-degree pool of water in a
backstroke position. Only my face protruded from the water.
This went on almost every morning for about a year. This half-
awake, half-asleep state was always accompanied by a marked

ambivalence. Though I was cozy under the covers, the physical comfort was coupled with a deep ache of despair. I lay there in the midst of sleep paralysis while also being keenly aware of my inability to change myself.

In my studies, I'd begun to be convinced of the doctrine of election—though I didn't have a theological vocabulary for it yet. But there was a problem: I internalized a beautiful truth meant to comfort as a threat against my soul. My seeming inability to stop sinning, coupled with the misappropriation of the doctrine of election, translated in my mind as doubt over my salvation.[3] Maybe I was never part of the elect in the first place. There in the confines of my warm, comfortable bed, a spiritual battle raged in my heart and mind. Unlike the horror-filled night terrors of my younger years, these dark thoughts brought me to a more dangerous place. When you're little, giant snakes scaling the walls at night are scary. Despairing over whether God loves you in the face of an inability to be a good Christian is sheer terror.

All these years later I no longer have the night terrors or that awful, half-sleep state of spiritual despair. But it's not because something in life got better. Instead, the Life Coach Jesus, who was disappointed in me and leering over my bed with arms crossed and toe tapping while he waited for me to get my act together, disappeared. Fortunately, that Jesus turned out to be a figment of my imagination.

You see, this fake Jesus was so often preached to me in the churches I attended. Instead of introducing a Savior, they had a mascot who was nothing more than a spiritual tyrant. My heart resonated with the tyrant because it kept me wringing my hands in self-focus. Just the way I liked it.

Those unable to sidestep conditional spirituality will inevitably get crushed under the weight. Those with consciences prone to unhealthy levels of introspection (read: me) already understand their limitations. If spiritual progression is up to them, there's no hope. So as I lay in bed in that tortured, half-sleep state, I pondered the same question over and over again: *My Christian life is supposed to reflect character, but I have none and I haven't lived up to the owner's manual for life—so is my faith a fake?*

When this dark cloud loomed over me as a new Christian, I'd double down into deeper, more committed efforts and heartfelt personal devotions. I would raise my hands more during the song service and stick to my one-year Bible reading plan. Sometimes it meant getting born-again again; I had a turnstile experience of going up to the altar after church service to recommit my life to God again and again and again. Others who reach this point may choose to get re-baptized (a practice I'm personally not too keen on). As some of us have found, deeper spiritual commitment based on a to-do list doesn't work—it makes things worse. About five years into the Christian life I just wanted to sleep, but even that was getting ruined.

THE QUALITY OF OUR FAITH VS. THE OBJECT OF OUR FAITH

The problem with self-focused faith is that it locates hope in an internal quality we think we can get our hands on—a quality made possible by obeying the rules of an "owner's manual." This is faith in a *quality* of faith instead of our *object* of faith, Jesus Christ himself. When we begin measuring the quality of our faith, we will feel judged. Not only by the external expectations of others, but our own hearts condemn us (1 John 3:20). This self-condemnation is what happened to me as a brand-new Christian. I was looking for the validation of my faith within myself and not in what Jesus had done for me already outside of my own experience. Holy Spirit–led conviction is a gift, but our own spiritual introspection can easily become a morbid black hole, deadly to the believer. I was at an impasse. I needed an answer to the hollow ring of despair—only it never came. I'd lost at the spiritual game and saw no point in continuing to go to church. And mid-week small group? Forget it. What's the point in going when you're the only one that doesn't seem to have it together?

I've painted a rather bleak picture. If you can relate to this experience at all, it's because you, too, have been lured into a spiritual cul-de-sac. You've gotten a steady diet of only one part of the whole Christian message. You may hear the occasional good and glorious Jesus-saves stuff, but only on Easter Sunday or during the annual evangelical community outreach. Beyond that, it's just the same old suffocating messages of aim higher, keep a good attitude, pick yourself up again, and hold up your end of the bargain. Only it's not working anymore. You're pretty sure Jesus can save a sinner, but you're not so sure if he can save a Christian.[4] You're burnt out, cynical, despairing.

The thing is, I had good reason for despairing, especially after I'd given up church for a while. I had really and truly failed at the Christian life, and the churches I attended during that time sent a message that I didn't belong there because I had problems—non-Christian type problems that I couldn't seem to shake. There was no place to process what I was experiencing, no place (it seemed) to receive forgiveness. When I read that academic book that claimed Christianity was not about morality, something clicked. I didn't exactly understand it at the time, but it rang true according to my experiences.

Christianity *isn't* about my morality. It's about Jesus giving himself to me and to you because we're unable to make things right with God on our own. Christianity isn't about morality; it's about the power of unrelenting forgiveness and the comforting presence of the Spirit who goes with us and before us. Another word for this is *grace*. The conversation Mom and I had in the car that summer afternoon was deeply meaningful, but I didn't yet understand why. I probably barely understand now. It felt awkward to ponder at the time, but Christianity is not about morality. When we make it about morality, we are set up for pride or despair. Instead, the focal point of

Christianity is Jesus Christ. We fall in love with him again and again because of his grace to sinners—to us.

DON'T SETTLE FOR JESUS-Y ADVICE

Here's what's obvious. Of course you and I should be getting better at the Christian life. Of course you and I should be more kind, loving, and generous. We do need to play by the rules of the "Owner's Manual for Life." Of course you should be making more of an impact in the world. You should feel really excited and energized in your faith. We all should. All God's demands are good, but the problem is, all the demanding isn't helping any of our doing. I don't know about you, but the exhortation to live a transformed life doesn't have an ounce of power to get me out of bed each morning.

If you've been told that the core of the Christian faith is your ongoing transformation by making good on all the Jesus-y advice, you're getting ripped off. Save yourself the heartache and peruse the self-help aisle instead. But if you have an inkling that the Christian life has something deeper to offer, you're onto something.

The fact is—and this has to be received in faith—God is making all things new despite whether you are willing or able to cooperate with him. Those who are in Christ, those who belong to Jesus possess a glorious already-not-yet present. Yes, we are called to express our faith in love, but don't forget that faith is God's gift. That good gift is not based on your ability to perform for him. You're in the family. You're adopted, loved, and secure.

Many of us have been hearing the one-note monotone[5] of Christian duty our entire lives, but the Christian message isn't music until we hear that second, all-important triumphant note of the gospel of Jesus Christ *for us*! Otherwise, the one note of the law inevitably drones on and accuses you as you lay in bed in a half-sleep state each morning. It reminds you over and over that you haven't lived life according to the owner's manual. You'll be forced to lug your shame around throughout the day. The shame and the accusations that accompany it linger. They'll climb into bed with you at night with their yellow, cold, pokey toenails and keep droning on into your ear like a bad case of nightmarish tinnitus. They say "do, do, do," but the work is never done.

The good news is that there is an antidote to the pride and despair, but it's severe. And while the Holy Spirit is a comforter, he'll lead us into circumstances where we get knocked around a bit. We might get a blackened eye or scraped knees. But I promise you, this antidote has the power to get us out of the mess of pride and despair.

Part II

The Antidote to Pride and Despair

Chapter 6
God's Law

A sergeant told a grim joke to his trainees during the
Second World War, which shows the real flaw in the
Pharisaic understanding of Christianity. A man stopped
on a dirt road to help get another man's car out of the
ditch. The latter was beginning to harness two small furry
kittens to the bumper of this huge car when he was asked,
"Mister, you aren't going to try to get those kittens to pull
that car out of the ditch, are you?" His reply was, "Why
not? I've got a whip." The lash of the Law is used in similar
spiritual situations. Without the principle of forgiveness
our conscience acquires a quality of cruelty that makes the
Gospel of Christ anything but the Good News.[1]

In the last chapter, I described a church congregation that sat
under heavy preaching. Recall again the underlying message:
first, get your life in order according to a specific lifestyle template; second, start volunteering time at the church; and third,
become a rock-star spouse and parent. OK, now imagine that
scene again.

After these types of sermons, there was a routine exhortation: get excited for all that Jesus had done and respond joy-
fully in the song service. It was a tough sell to the congregation
because we'd just received a fifty-minute verbal bulldoze. We
were stuck in an awkward place. We knew a joyful response was
in order. God is good. He sent Jesus to die for sin so we would
receive new life. But the monotone of the heavy-handedness

droned on for months and years. Over time it became a dull ache that never quite resolved in any spiritual comfort. There had to be a way out of the heaviness, but the weightiness seemed to cling to us. The joy-filled response was a stretch rather than authentic.

Explicit Message versus Implied Message

All the ingredients of faithful preaching were present in the sermons we heard on Sundays. We had heard God's rightful demand to live holy lives. The messages were tailored to help the congregation identify aspects of life not squaring with God's command. So far, so good. Next, we heard the good news of the gospel. Jesus saves sinners and redeems the brokenness of our lives. Great. It was the next move that was the spiritual death knell: get on mission and live a transformed life. The flow of the message went something like this: "You are not living up to God's demands. Look at all that Jesus has done for you, and now get to work. Oh, and get excited about it and clap during the praise service, you bunch of deadbeats!"

The doctrine of justification by faith was explicit enough. The problem was the implied message (don't be a consumer in church—serve, and get your life together) crowded out the explicit message of *forgiveness and redemption, no strings attached.* The result was a conflicted communication that highlighted achievement over forgiveness. While the communication was clear—the message was concise, compelling, funny, entertaining, and witty—the takeaway was not the good news of what Jesus had done for sinners like you and me. It was more like "Get to work for Jesus." Again, this is *not* the gospel message.

The Gospel Message as a Means to an End

A Sunday morning message can include a lot of talk about Jesus or a whole bunch of Bible teaching. But when the transformed life of the believer takes center stage in the pulpit, you've got a problem. In such a setting, the message of "For freedom Christ has set us free" (Galatians 5:1) gets perverted to mean "earn your keep." Maybe I'm just a softy, but forgiveness, love, and the comfort of our Savior ought to be the high point of a church service. When this message becomes a means to an end (such as mobilizing volunteers to build a megachurch), it becomes a muddled if not false message.

Transformed-life preaching comes in many varieties. This type of preaching proclaims a variety of different Christs: Life Coach Jesus, Checklist Jesus, Movement Leader Jesus, Visionary Jesus, and each hold out big promises to the hearer based on a variation of the "Owner's Manual for Life." The sermons include the common threads of commands, exhortations, attaboys, encouragement to get on mission, and brags about the church growth. When this happens, the gospel takes a back seat. Hearers are left with moralism that takes the air right out of the room.

There are many examples of this type of preaching from the pulpit: The Gospel-Afterthought, the Gospel Sandwich, and the Life Application.[2] Take for instance the Gospel-Afterthought—the kind of Christian talk that hurriedly tacks a gospel message to the end of a sermon. If you blink, you might just miss it. Or there's the Gospel Sandwich, which is the kind of sermon that makes you feel like salvation is dependent on your obedience. The last word of these sermons is usually a list of the dos and don'ts of the Christian life. Then there's the most popular of all, the Life Application Sermon. This sermon claims the Bible as God's owner's manual for life. The idea is that the Bible shows us how we should live. Somehow Jesus's words in John 5:39 that the Scripture is all about him get turned around. The words that testify about him get perverted to mean they're the words that testify about you.[3]

This is not free grace coming from our Savior. Life Coach Jesus and all the other less-than saviors remind us that "there are no free lunches. You get what you give." The Gospel Sandwich and the Life Application messages leave you feeling like you need to hurry up and get to work for God in order to be OK—and when you don't succeed there is condemnation. The Gospel Afterthought is something you might hear Visionary Jesus espouse: "The gospel, well, yes, of course, but c'mon, let's get to the action. There's an empire to build here."

ACCESSING THE MOOD OF THE LIFE COACH, CHECKLIST, MOVEMENT LEADER, AND VISIONARY JESUS MESSAGE

The "Jesus as life coach" type of Christianity has a mood that is not always easy to identify. Often the environment includes a good bit of talk about Jesus, but the takeaway of the message is most definitely not "Jesus paid it all." After listening to a message like this, you're probably confused by the time you get to your car. Here's how it goes: You go to a church service. The pastor is well spoken, knows the Bible, and loves the people in the pews. Biblical truths are taught, and you feel challenged to live more wholeheartedly for Christ. You may even learn something interesting from the Bible that you didn't know before. After the service, you say your pleasantries to other church folk while you drink a bad cup of coffee. By the time you get back to your car, the gospel has vanished. You get situated in your seat, clasp your seat belt, check your mirrors, and drive away. Then the sermon takeaway comes to mind. But the message is not "Jesus loves you and forgives you." It's more like "Here's one more chance. Don't blow this." Between the church's front door and your car, the good news has dissipated into the ether. In this situation, the Transformed Christian Life has taken center stage and not Jesus who died for sinners. Sure, Jesus is central to this message, but only as a means to an end.

If you're feeling confused about your standing with God after a sermon, there is a good chance you have heard a sermon principally based on what you must do. This is a law-based sermon rather than a gospel sermon.

I recall this uneasy feeling after hearing a sermon a few short years ago. Our church was in the middle of a long series on marriage. On the drive home I always felt like I'd just wasted an hour of my life. Don't get me wrong. Good marriage advice is invaluable, especially if you and your spouse are struggling. My wife and I have received good counsel from wise pastors and leaders in the past, and we have appreciated it very much. But is a Sunday church service the best place for this kind of message?

I remember sitting with a friend a few years ago who was devastated and crying with mascara running down her cheeks. She was a young, anxious mother, and she was convinced she could never be a domestic hero like the pastor's wife. Though the message was advice on how to be a good wife and mother, all she could hear was the accusation that she wasn't adding up. Mothering and marriage opinions and advice have a place. But in the church nothing should take top billing over the proclamation of the gospel.

It seems to me that the most important thing a pastor has to share with people in the pews is Jesus, his forgiveness of sin, and his proclamation that God is renewing all things in the world. We need to hear Scripture, sing songs together, and partake of communion. I can get sound marriage advice down at the local bookstore, or by seeing a trained psychologist, or even during a teaching hour at church. On Sunday I need to hear a message I'm not going to hear anywhere else. Occasional life tips in a sermon may be fine, but an entire month-long series? This sort of pulpit advice often says do more, be more, achieve more. Fit the mold. The Law of God to love your neighbor gets presented as steps for life success. And when you're unable to fit the mold, what does that say about you? Have I loved God with my whole heart, soul, mind, and strength and my neighbor as myself? No, I have not. Therefore, what I most need when I go to church is a reminder of forgiveness and our great Savior who loves me unconditionally. This is what gives me the courage and motivation to go out and once again seek to love my God and my neighbor.

THE GOOD INTENTIONS OF ADVICE-DRIVEN CHRISTIANITY

The advice-oriented teaching I received in churches was meant to be helpful. Nobody was knowingly trying to deceive me or the congregation. I'm sure that many of the popular Christian books on the shelves steeped in Christian-y advice come from well-intentioned authors. I believe the speaker on the tape series that got passed around at that little Pentecostal church I attended was well-intentioned too. The problem is that a message that hinges on what I must do can never be a good news message.

Maybe you're steadier than I am, but my heart is all over the place every single day. Some days are better than others. Some days I feel gratitude to God throughout the day. Some days I act lovingly toward my neighbor and spouse. Some days I feel like I'm contributing well to humanity with the gifts and talents God has given me. Other days, I feel like a clod, have a crappy attitude, wonder why God put me on the earth, and want to be left alone to binge-watch Netflix all day.

I don't know about you, but I need a Christian message that tells me something more than what I must do or who I must be. I have spiritual amnesia and have to hear the gospel over and over to keep centered. I'm convinced that when the message of grace and command, or law and gospel gets sloppy, it produces what we've already discussed: pride and despair. I've experienced it in my life firsthand, and I see it in others' lives all the time.

HOW GOD'S LAW WORKS

The true purpose of the Law is to kick our butts and show us our desperate need for Jesus. The Law is not good news.

It's a death sentence and a never-ending accusation. The Law imprisons us and puts us under guarded watch (Galatians 3:23–24). This is not to disparage the Law. As Paul says in Romans, the Law is holy, righteous, and good (7:12). The Law isn't the problem; we are the problem because we can't live up to its demands.

The law has two uses: civic and theological. The civic use—referred to as the second use—is the day-to-day law on the street: speed limits, consequences for crime, the boundaries that mark our society as civil. For example, it's important to stop at a red light so you don't flatten that mother and her baby she's pushing in a stroller across the street. And if you can't restrain yourself from running red lights, there is a punishment waiting for you in the form of a traffic violation. These kinds of laws restrain evil so that the world is a better place to live. This is the "second use" of the law.

The "first use" (or theological/spiritual use) is what drives us to Jesus.[4] The law is ". . . a real 'voice' which 'sounds in the heart' and the 'conscience,' a real voice which afflicts man in his isolation from God and demands that he fulfill his humanity."[5] When this dynamic of the law is at work, we know when we're guilty, and almost anything—either real or perceived—will condemn us. A friend or your spouse gives you a sideways look. Hearing a sermon you're convinced was meant specifically to call you on a specific sin. This voice of the law can come from anywhere, even ". . . the rustling of the leaves on a dark night in a strange place. . . [It] frightens us because, I suppose we could say, we do not have life in ourselves and something—anything—'out there' can take it from us."[6] But the Law has its limits; it's a one-trick pony with a particular function. Imagine frosting a cake with a hammer. I suppose you could kind of get the job done. But it's the wrong tool for the work at hand. The Law rattles our cages. Better yet, we need the Law's full force to get us good and dead—dead to our own selfishness, blindness, and perpetual sin. The Law cannot save. It condemns, judges, accuses, reviles, kills, and brings wrath. These are the Bible's words by the way, not mine.

This concept of the Law may seem harsh or negative, but for me, it was one piece of an overall message that caused my faith to brim with hope for the first time in years. This is because the Law tees things up for the reception of the good news of the gospel. After all, how is good news good unless we have an understanding of bad news? We've got to hear a diagnosis before we are offered the cure.

LOWERCASE "L" LAW

Beyond the Bible's definition of Law, you could say there are the lesser, lowercase "l" laws of life. This is the nagging voice everyone lugs around with them in their heart and conscience. It's the voice that demands continual self-improvement. The lowercase "l" is the law that my friend and new mother experienced as she aspired to be a domestic rock star like the pastor's wife. Even lowercase "l" law terrorizes us: you can get spooked by a bolt of lightning in a storm, or someone you love gets hurt in a tragic accident.[7] It comes with the pushy demands of family, friends, or the tax man. It hides in the application section of a sermon.

The Law of God booming down on us from The Ten Commandments can seem somewhat ethereal. But we live with these lower "l" laws of life all the time. Maybe we can better understand our relationship to God's holy Law by looking at the little "l" laws in the everyday. Let's face it, everyday life often has the same sort of psychological impact:[8] the "thou shalts" of professional life, when you feel like you have to justify your existence with how many hours you put in at the office; the "thou shalts" of body image and the healthy choices of eating organic; not to mention the "thou shalts" of your social media feed, the things both visible to you and others used to measure and accuse you. It's helpful to diagnose the effects of the law with everyday life from a theological vantage point of human experience, from the bottom up.[9]

The Grammar of Law Lite

The proclamation of false Jesuses has a particular grammar to it. Life Coach Jesus says, if you are going to derive the benefits of law keeping, it's all up to you. The focus is on what you are doing. You are the subject of all the verbs. Movement Leader and Visionary Jesus say you must take the advice and get busy. You must get on mission and serve. Checklist Jesus says you must be transformed. You must discover your destiny. You must obey the rules of the owner's manual for life. You must get that one thing in your life under control and then you'll experience victory! You must be a better wife or a better husband. A steady diet of this stuff produces what we've said all along: pride or despair. It's inevitable. Pride when we have a checklist we're able to complete and feel satisfied with. Despair when we can't seem to fit the mold. As long as we're alive, the law has an infinite number of tactics and they all whisper, *You are not enough.*

Those of us who have sat at the feet of the false Jesuses have come to believe the myth that the lesser version of the owner's manual would somehow deliver positive outcomes. All the false Jesuses (Life Coach Jesus, Visionary Jesus, Movement Leader Jesus, and Checklist Jesus) are all singing a monotone law-lite chorus. But often this monotone note casts a spell that keeps us from becoming completely dead. Instead, we're saddled up with demands to the point of death and placed on life support to hang on for dear life. It would be more humane for a preacher to preach the full counsel of God, demand and law in its full undiluted, crushing form, and let that word put people out of their misery. Instead, we get new checklists, and we're put back on life support again. It's a vicious cycle.

THE KILLING FUNCTION OF THE LAW

In reality, God's unbridled Law doesn't wrap you up in a Snuggie of God's love. It picks you up by the scruff of the neck and kicks your butt all the way around the block. God's Law does not offer life; it bludgeons you. It doesn't offer comfort; it points an accusing, ten-foot bony finger in your face. It wakes you up in the morning in a half-sleep state and gets you to wonder, *My life is a mess. Am I even a Christian?* The Law is merciless. It doesn't let you off the hook and give you a pat on the back; it judges your every move. It doesn't come to save, but to condemn and throw you in prison. And to top it off, as you strive to be righteous in your own Christian good deeds, the irony is that you're put off course. You end up miles from the original goal. Once you've set out to keep your nose clean and be a good Christian, you find yourself miles from shore. You're treading water, but losing stamina fast. Then Life Coach Jesus comes traipsing across the water, and hands you a couple ten-pound barbells.[10]

The point of all this doom-and-gloom talk about the Law is to tease out what the purpose of the Law truly is. It kills. It accuses. It curses everything that is not in Christ. And when it gets you good and dead, it has done its job properly. Then it's time for a completely different word: the word of the gospel.

There has been much debate for centuries over these issues, and I won't even come close to scratching the surface here. But for what it's worth, beginning to understand the basic grammar of the Law and gospel distinction has been transformative to my personal faith life. To me, it corresponds to the realities and life, and it has given me a grammar that makes sense of the world—my world anyway.

I am no scholar, but given the trustworthy, thoughtful scholarship I've read on the subject and reading Scripture carefully myself, I've come to the conclusion that the Law and gospel distinction is all over the Bible, in both the Old Testament and the New Testament. The Law and gospel distinction is a Reformational hallmark on both the Lutheran as well as the Reformed side. There are certainly differences in theological emphasis, but the core agreement is stronger than the issues that divide. A careful reading of both Luther and Calvin as well as Lutheran and Reformed confessions demonstrates that there is a core message pertaining to the distinction of Law and gospel.

What it all comes down to for me is that ultimately, the Law (the Ten Commandments, the Sermon on the Mount, and the lowercase "l" laws in everyday life) accuses and crushes because no one lives up to it. No matter how hard we try, we cannot live up to the totality of the demands of the Law—all of the laws. The summary of the Law is to love God with your whole heart, soul, body, and mind. How's that working out for you? And, as to add insult to injury, the Law also requires you to love your neighbor as yourself. I don't know about you, but I have a hard time loving my family, much less my neighbor.

Because we all fail to love perfectly, functionally the Law accuses us. We have not and cannot live up to its demand, and yet the Law is still there holding up the mirror to show me my sin and failure. This is a good thing though because we know this is still God's will for life. The Law shows us what is good for us and for our neighbor. It reveals God's holy character. And it reveals "you ain't got it." That's the bad news. The good news is that there is a gospel for that. That is, Jesus fully and completely fulfilled the Law in our place. He died for our sins and was raised for our justification. When we fail to keep and obey the Law, we look again to Jesus for forgiveness and the empowering Holy Spirit to enable us to love God and our neighbor as we ought.

When it comes to Law, we have this innate tendency to see the Law almost as a staircase we must climb to get to God. But this is an "up the down staircase" strategy.[11] Human beings don't set out on a spiritual adventure where they climb to God. He condescends and comes down to them, to us. The

Christian life isn't a climb to spiritual excellence and achievement; it's a pattern of death and resurrection. Repentance and forgiveness. This is the circular pattern of the Christian life. Where the Law has said "do this and live" (and it never gets done), Jesus says, "I have done it all," and the believer rests in that finished work. Repentance and forgiveness, repentance and forgiveness until we get that big old dirt nap. As we've said all along, God deals in death and resurrections, so it's all going to work out.

THE FUNCTION OF GOD'S LAW IN SCRIPTURE

Let's take a look at a few Bible passages on the purpose and function of God's Law to reinforce what has been said thus far. First we'll look at the Law from the Old Testament, then from the teaching of Jesus, and finally from the words of the apostle Paul. This examination is not exhaustive by any stretch. It is more an observation of the dynamic of what the Law does to people according to Scripture. My trajectory is to show that in the final analysis, in Paul's theology the Law's function is to kill (Romans 7:10), accuse (Romans 2:15), and judge (Romans 2:12). Again, the Bible's words, not mine.

Law in the Old Testament

At the time of the giving of the Ten Commandments, God had destroyed the Israelites' enemies. In love, he led the people out of Egyptian captivity. Again and again God reassures the people, "I am the LORD your God, who brought you out of the land of Egypt, out of the house of slavery" (Exodus 20:2). This love was a father/son relational love; this was the context of the giving of the Law: a loving relationship with his people. That sounds great. But read the narrative itself. Pay attention to the response of the Israelites after the giving of the Ten Commandments.[12]

Now when all the people saw the thunder and the flashes of lightning and the sound of the trumpet and the mountain smoking, the people were afraid and trembled, and they stood far off and said to Moses, "You speak to us, and we will listen; but do not let God speak to us, lest we die." (Exodus 20:18-19)

The Israelites were in the presence of utter, holy perfection. But it doesn't read like a spiritual edification and cozy time with God. It was a little more like a scene from a horror and suspense flick. The people were all soiling their tunics in the presence of God. They couldn't even go near the mountain. Instead they cowered in the opening of their tents and watched from a distance when Moses went up to meet God. This was not a mountaintop experience as memorialized on motivational posters we see hanging in corporate hallways. The brutal truth is that if people drew near to the mountain, they were toast.

Jesus Comes Along and Makes Matters Worse!

OK, so the giving of the Law was scary. Hmm, maybe gentle Jesus reframed things to round off the hard edges. After all, he extended grace, and he didn't add any new commands. But to understand the function of the Law, we'd do well to get Jesus's take straight from Scripture. If you read the text, Jesus seems to actually make matters worse for his hearers, not better.

Think for a moment about the weightiness of the Sermon on the Mount. We have to contend with "You therefore must be perfect, as your heavenly father is perfect" (Matthew 5:48) —and all that goes with it. There is the hard to swallow "go the extra mile" (Matthew 5:41) and "turn the other cheek" (Matthew 5:39). Now, let's be honest. How's that's going for you? If some thug made you carry their satchel for a mile under threat, you wouldn't be glad to go another mile. You'd be looking for a police car to flag down, tattle on the guy, and get him thrown in jail.

Say you were at the corner coffee shop minding your own business. You trip on an awkwardly placed rug and spill latte foam on the lapel of someone's new polo shirt. You get in a brawl out of no fault of your own and receive a smack to the face. You would not be glad to offer the other side to get rearranged for the sake of facial symmetry. Someone tough might dish it back out. The weaklings among us would curl up into a ball on the floor to protect themselves. Or how about this: pay attention to your heart rate the next time you watch the evening news. When the talking head rambles on about a political issue you disagree with, take notice. You feel like calling them an idiot, don't you? Oops. Too bad, you're in danger of hellfire (Matthew 5:22).

Now, do you have any enemies, like, real enemies? Think about all the ways you have loved them in the ways you love yourself. I'll bet out of the goodness of your heart you sent them a gift card to the spa and a box of chocolates last week. And they're at the top of your prayer journal list. No? I didn't think so.

And yet, these demands are the content of the Sermon on the Mount. Here's how the basic flow of it goes. Before the Sermon on the Mount, in Matthew 4:17, Jesus says, "Repent, for the kingdom of heaven is at hand." As he leads into the sermon, he tells his hearers to turn from what they are doing now and go the other way. Change your mind. This tends to be the ordinary flow of Scripture. We have to contend with the rightful, holy demand before receiving a word of pardon.

Next comes the Beatitudes. Some of the Beatitudes are comforting enough. Blessed are the poor, blessed are the persecuted for my sake, blessed are those who mourn. Blessed are the underdogs. But then Jesus lays out another kind of list. Blessed are the merciful, the meek, the pure in heart. Ask yourself how merciful, meek, and pure of heart you have been today. How'd it go last week? How merciful, meek, and pure is enough?

Then Matthew 5:20 follows, "For I tell you, unless your righteousness exceeds that of the scribes and Pharisees, you will never enter the kingdom of heaven." Dang, this is getting too hot to handle. We all love to turn the Pharisees into punching bags, but these guys were the real deal. They were up before the rooster crows and on their knees praying. They were tithing ten percent of everything they had, including from the spices and herb garden. These were no spiritual slouches. Now Jesus says to be more righteous than those guys. Wait. *What?*

A few things of note. Jesus was purposefully uncovering the deeper meaning of the Ten Commandments. Watch the clues. He ascended the mountain and said, "You have heard it said, but I say . . ." In doing this, he redefined the Law itself. He was saying, "Hey guys, you know how Moses went to a mountain for the commandments? Check me out. I'm on a mountain too. Know how you have heard since you were a kid the commandments of Moses? Well, maybe that's what you've heard, but here's what *I* say." You might think at that point Jesus would loosen up on the Law. Instead, he tightened it to the extreme. Just when you think you're going to get a lucky break with Jesus and maybe get a high five, he makes things worse. He crawls into your head and judges your very motives and thoughts. Dang.

On a good day, you might be able to refrain from flipping off the person who cuts you off in traffic. You might mutter "fiddlesticks" instead of another four-letter word in your vocabulary. You might decide to say nothing when you can't say anything nice. You may even squeeze out a perfunctory prayer for that unlovable son-of-a-gun down the street who starts his mower at 7 a.m. on Saturday mornings. But c'mon. You and I have flunked the test already. This is Jesus telling us what a good and holy life ought to look like, but none of us is living up to the standard. Maybe we can get by on the ABCs of Ten Commandments rule keeping, at least as far as outward behavior goes. Jesus goes right for the jugular of the inner life, where thoughts and desires are born. Our sin runs deep—so deep that our outward behavior can't undo it.

On the surface of things, Jesus's main points in the Sermon on the Mount seem like an exercise in futility. Why did he tell people to do something they have no chance in hell to pull off? I know there is much debate among scholars about this. Maybe Jesus is outlining an ethical program for believers. I'm not sure I agree. To my mind, Jesus is creating a crisis for his hearers. They weren't performing any better with Law abiding than you or me. Our sin, our selfishness, our pettiness, our self-pity, and our everyday sloppiness has no bounds. We are completely incapable of helping ourselves when it comes to sin management. Consider all the everyday instances we've covered—the fouled-mouthed commute to work and the hate in your heart against that idiot politician. Now measure it against the heavy-handed stuff Jesus talks about in the Sermon on the Mount. We don't even come close to coming out even. Well, maybe there are other parts of the Bible that can help us sort things through.

According to the Apostle Paul, the Law Equals Death

Keep in mind that Paul was a Pharisee of Pharisees. He knew the Law. I've heard some folks object to the crushing function of the Law. They wisely point out how important context is and remind us that we have to understand how the original hearers received it. I've heard some say that the negative press the Law often gets is misguided.[13]

It's not as though the confusion surrounding Paul's use of the Law is unwarranted. I've thought to myself at times that there seems to be a disconnect between the sternness of Jesus in the Gospels and the sayings of Paul about love and grace. Some want to jettison Paul in favor of the red letters of Scripture, but this is a mistake. Paul explains what Jesus did.[14] That is, Paul lays out in theological detail what Jesus lived out in real life, in real time with sinners like you and me. That's the beauty of the canon of Scripture.

At the risk of oversimplifying, imagine the Gospels are the movie of Jesus's life, death, resurrection, and ascension as told by those who were there in real time. The Epistles then are like the play-by-play explanation of all that went into the making of the movie. An explanation of the meaning of recurring phrases and scenes. At some point all analogies fall apart, but think of the heavy, systematic theology in Paul's Epistles as the behind the scenes in-the-studio commentary.

There is much that could be said about Paul's Law and gospel theology. The debates have raged for millennia. I don't have anything new to add here. In fact, I am only calling attention to a theological framework that has existed for a long time. When it comes to the purpose and function of the Law, I'm going with the apostle Paul on this one. He had very strong convictions on the purpose and function of the Law, and that it was distinct from the gospel. Paul clearly outlines the purpose and function in Galatians and Romans. He called the Law a curse for anyone who did not obey it (Galatians 3:10). He said the Law brought wrath (Romans 4:15), and death (Romans 7:10). He referred to the Law as a judge (Romans 2:12) and those who boast in the Law as dishonoring God by breaking the Law (Romans 2:23).

In the end, whether it's uppercase "L" Law or the lesser lowercase "l" laws, the result is similar. Life is a treadmill, and you will never be finished. The Law takes prisoners, but no one gets out alive; it's going to take you out along with every other soul on God's good green earth. There is sweet rest awaiting us, but it's not a promise found in the Law. If you look there, it will be an exercise as futile as smashing your head against a brick wall.

CONCLUSION

As I mentioned in the introduction, I am aware that even within these pages, I am as susceptible as anyone to "get Jesus wrong" again. If I'm fortunate enough to receive a review or two of this book, I can imagine critical reviewers using the title to point out just how "wrong" I really am! It's not like I believe my faith has arrived because I found some dusty theological puzzle pieces hiding under the couch. And further, getting all the theological ducks in a row could just as easily be another one of those false Jesuses. You see, even a correct view of the Law and gospel hermeneutic could keep me away from the embrace of the real Jesus who lived, bled, died, and resurrected for me and you. I do believe that good theology is meant to point us to Christ, but theology is never an end in itself. As always, Robert Farrar Capon puts it as well as anyone ever could. He said theology is like a porch to a house. The point of a porch is to get someone into the house of faith of what Jesus has done—died and raised for sinners.

Capon goes on to say that the porch builder at one time had a simple sturdy porch. Then he tore it down and rebuilt it with ornate decorations. On evenings when the weather is good, he throws wine and cheese parties to entertain friends. At some point, the porch builder's wife comes along. She says, "This porch is falling into disrepair. It's more trouble than it's worth. Tear it down, and we'll just hoist ourselves up into the house like the days before we had a porch."

Inevitably, believing people have a porch on their home of faith. It's also possible to have a gaudy porch and not spend time in the house. The point is that there's a house we need to get into. Here's the conundrum: the only way to get someone to the front door is across that porch. It's true that theologizing never saved anybody. But that porch lies between everybody and the Saving Proposition Himself.[15]

This may be an apt description of the Law/gospel distinction. I'm of the belief that "Law and gospel" is all over

Scripture. It's a good, sturdy, simple porch, and it has gotten many of us into the house of faith in Jesus. If you're not in full agreement, at least it gets me into the house of faith. I hope it can get you there too. This is where death and resurrection is at the heart of Christianity itself.

Chapter 7
God's Gospel

Imagine you're spending time with a friend at a coffee shop. You're both casually perusing the newspaper, and your friend mentions a headline about a miracle cure for a rare disease. It would be pleasant, passing information, but likely not the hot topic of conversation. You'd politely nod, smile, and go back to nursing your beverage.

Now consider a different scenario: You've had puzzling health problems. You toss and turn most nights in a cold sweat. During the day you're experiencing the most excruciating headaches you've ever known. You can't concentrate in meetings, and you've lost your appetite. At the insistence of your spouse, you finally go see another doctor. You've been in and out of the doctor's office for invasive testing. Sadly, the diagnosis has turned utterly grim: you have a terminal disease without a cure. You are going to die, and soon.

Imagine the devastation of this news. Grief sets in as you await the inevitable. You can't sleep, you can't eat, and no one can snap you out of your despair. You wait in your hospital bed for that next wince of pain, wondering if it will be your last. Suddenly, your doctor barges into the hospital room holding a medical journal and pointing to a headline. Scientists have discovered a surefire cure for your disease, and you can start treatment immediately! To be at death's door and to hear about a miraculous, lifesaving medical cure would cause a joy-filled response.[1]

So it is with God's Law and the gospel. When we don't clearly understand the truth of a diagnosis (your disease is terminal, there's no present cure), the good news of a cure doesn't make much sense. The Law and gospel must always go together, but they have different functions. One kills, and the other makes alive. One is the diagnosis, the other is the cure. And Law is always in service to the gospel. One theologian from the late 1800s put it well—without this distinction of Law and gospel, "scripture is and remains a closed book."[2] Further on he said, "Rightly distinguishing the Law and the Gospel is the most difficult and the highest art of Christians in general and of theologians in particular. It is taught only by the Holy Spirit in the school of experience."[3] At the time of the Reformation, John Calvin's successor, Theodore Beza, had a similar thought. He said, ". . . ignorance of this distinction between Law and Gospel is one of the principle sources of the abuses which corrupted and still corrupt Christianity." This is not a small fringe theological subject, and it is often not well understood.

GOD'S GAME-CHANGING THREE-LETTER WORD

One of the very best chunks of Scripture to consider on the distinction of Law and gospel is in Romans chapters 1 through 3. In those three short chapters, Paul demonstrates that everyone is imprisoned as breakers of the Law. Whether they are religious, or non-religious, whether they are Jew or Gentile. The Law nails every single person to the wall. No exception. Then there is a transition in the text at Romans 3:21. It's a three-letter word with all the significance in the world behind it. The word is "but." It's the signal that God has come on the scene and is changing the game. Let's read the passage.

> Now we know that whatever the law says it speaks
> to those who are under the law, so that every mouth
> may be stopped, and the whole world may be held

accountable to God. For by works of the law no human being will be justified in his sight, since through the law comes knowledge of sin. *But* now the righteousness of God has been manifested apart from the law, although the Law and the Prophets bear witness to it—the righteousness of God through faith in Jesus Christ for all who believe. (Romans 3:19–22, emphasis added)

The Law shuts everyone's mouth and makes every single soul accountable to God. No human being is justified in themselves.

Notice the glorious word *but*. BUT now God is doing something new in Jesus Christ. And this, dear Christian, is your glorious hope. Hang on to Jesus. Believe him. Trust him. He is the resurrection and the life. When the Law takes you out with that one-two punch—as it does—Jesus will stand you back up and say, "I forgive you. Let's go." When the problems of life come and go—and they will—the Law and death are never ever, ever the last words. Even when you keel over and die, it's not the last word. Jesus is the last word. And he has done it all. He has conquered all. He has risen indeed, and he's taking you with him.

Coming to terms with the proper function of Law and gospel has been good news for my soul. It means that all that I've experienced as God's "no" (Law) has an answer in the gospel of Jesus (God's "yes").[4] It means there has been a way out of the weightiness after all! Even the softer owner's manual for life law has run its course and closed off all exits to me. I've found that the law, by itself, can't produce life in me. It just makes me good and dead.

So now, twenty-five years into this Christianity thing, I'm crying "uncle!" I'm done. I'm tapped out. I'm crushed. But this isn't the last word. The gospel is the last word. I am justified by God in the present tense.

And even more than this, he's not done with me. There's a glimpse of something greater, far-off on the horizon, a future resurrection and glorification. As it says in 1 John 3:2, "When he appears we shall be like him, because we shall see him as he is." Even more mind melting, Peter says we will "become partakers of the divine nature" (2 Peter 1:4). Most days I can barely see it through the haze, but if I squint, it's like I can faintly see hope on the horizon. I believe I can change in this lifetime because I'm told in Romans 6:4 that I'm baptized into Jesus's death. "We were buried therefore with him by baptism into death, in order that, just as Christ was raised from the dead by the glory of the Father, we too might walk in newness of life." And though I can't always see this newness of life with any clarity, I'll hold on for dear life to that death and resurrection with Christ.

In part, I hope this means my wife doesn't have to be married to a defensive, cold, shut-down caveman forever. But even if I botch this, it means that God will bring me— and all Christians everywhere from all times and places—to his kingdom where he will dry every eye. And on account of what Christ has done for me and for you he will say, "Well done, good and faithful servant." Like the prodigal son who selfishly used up his father's inheritance, like the elder brother who pouted because he didn't feel adequately celebrated, God says to me and to you, "All that I have is yours." I don't know about you, but some days this makes me want to fist-pump the sky in Rocky Balboa victory. God's not done, friends! He's just not. So when the little deaths of life, and the inevitable capital "D" death shows up on the front step, we can rest assured that the death the Law brings is not the last word. This gives me hope. And I can use all the hope I can get. I bet you can too. As one host from the Thinking Fellows podcast has put it, "hope comes to us on the lips of another."[5]

Ideas Have Consequences

Can you recall a time in your life when someone has said something to you that changed the way you saw the world?

Sadly, these moments can be harsh words said when we're young that hang on into adulthood. At other times a word of encouragement comes to us from a friend, or we're challenged to see things from a different point of view by a good teacher. Maybe you were reading the Bible when God spoke to you through a particular verse. I've experienced these moments too, and one stands out from the last couple years.

A few years ago, I was preparing to teach at a recovery ministry event. A fellow leader and I were discussing some nuances on how I could best communicate a key point. This may seem a bit obscure, but he shared a phrase from the Protestant Reformation that forever shifted my thinking.[6] These words have both haunted my theological point of view and given me great comfort ever since. It's the crescendo statement of Martin Luther's Heidelberg Disputation, "God's love does not find, but creates, that which is pleasing to it." I know it sounds like something Yoda would say, but read it again slowly. Let it seep into your bones.

What does it mean? Think about it this way. We are drawn to attractive things or people that will benefit us in some way. Human love centers on the idea that we love something (or someone) because of how we can benefit from the relationship. And things that benefit us are pleasing. This is how we fall in love with our own image. We imagine others existing to somehow make our lives better for us, and we project that image onto God. We imagine God as a means to our ends, and in the process we falsify Jesus's identity into mere coach, manager, movement leader, visionary, checklist giver or _____ (fill in the blank).

But God doesn't find us doing a bunch of God stuff, decide that he likes what he sees, and then give us a reward. Instead, God turns the tables on this whole economy of finding beauty and purpose in people. He creates beauty by setting his sights on what is not lovely and pleasing and makes us pleasing by loving us.

In the beginning he created out of nothing (ex nihilo) with words. This creation out of nothing is considered a "speech act." "Speech act" means that when God speaks, things happen. The world came into being, but Jesus also calmed the storm with a word (Matthew 8:23–27). He told a paralytic to take up his mat and walk (John 5:8). He called to dead Lazarus to come forth, out of his tomb (John 11:43). So when Jesus says our sins won't be held against us (the proclamation of absolution), this is a "speech act" that accomplishes the goal of the words themselves. Forgiveness from God happens in real space and time, and people are forgiven and taken from death to life. God does two things with his word: he kills and he makes alive. His word is both a hammer and a salve (Deuteronomy 32:39; 1 Samuel 2:6). Hearing the two words of death and life is how faith is created in us. We experience a death by the word of the Law (the hammer), and resurrection to new life in Christ alone by the word of the gospel (the salve).

Hammers and salves have different and distinct functions. As we've seen in the last chapter, hammers don't have healing properties, and it doesn't work well when you use one to spread frosting on a cake. A salve is meant to heal, not crush. This is the distinction of command and promise, Law and gospel, life and death.

God doesn't find all the law abiders in the world and decide to return the favor with his blessing. That is reward, not grace. Grace is only grace when it's undeserved and unearned. Grace is pure gift with zero strings attached. *Ze-ro.* God's love does not find, but it creates that which is pleasing to it. That has a ring to it, doesn't it? God loves the unlovely. He doesn't find your good qualities; he creates them out of nothing with no help from you. Now THAT is good news.

Once God's Law has finished swinging its wrecking ball, God comes in and speaks life in Christ. He brings good news, forgiveness, pardon, and an eternal promise. Those who trust Jesus with their sin and failure are always and forever in the "In Club." When Jesus enlivens us with faith through his words, when we hear God's yes in Jesus, we're no longer excluded. We're "in," prodigal-son-returned-home in.

God answers death with resurrection. *Gospel* literally means "good news," a definitive statement of an accomplished fact. What news? News about what has been done on behalf of you and me through Jesus Christ. Through Christ we are given a grace-filled Christianity, one focused on the high point of the gospel with an altogether different "no" grammar than the Law—no condemnation, no fear, no death. In all the activity of the Christian life, listen carefully to the verbiage. Ask the question, Who is the subject of the action words? The answer should be Jesus. Jesus bled and died for you. You don't have to expire blood, sweat, and tears for him. Jesus rose from the grave for you. You don't raise yourself from the ashes to be counted worthy for him. Jesus gives us the Holy Spirit, we don't call the Spirit down. Yes, we are to live holy lives; Jesus is Lord and King and he demands our faithfulness. But the difference between the life coach, checklist giver, movement leader, and visionary Jesuses and the Jesus of the Bible is the difference between "you must do" and "he has done." "The Law says 'do this' and is never done. The gospel says 'believe in this,' and everything is already done."[7]

In the past, I've been entranced by the message of the false Jesuses. Turns out, all the false Jesuses were taskmasters. Checklist Jesus only knew how to dole out checklists, which put me on an unending hamster wheel. Visionary Jesus promised great things: belonging to a movement of God and "building the kingdom" alongside a group of exceptional believers connected to an exceptional leader. But many leaders bitten by this bug tend toward narcissism and end up grinding up their followers. (I've seen it firsthand.) Movement Leader Jesus promised great spiritual experiences. But the experiences only came along about as often as a lunar eclipse. And when they did happen, I didn't know if it was substantial or was indigestion from the burrito the night before. I may never know.

Maybe I chased after these lesser gods because it gave me a clear template to follow in life. The problem came when I realized that the commands of these make-believe Jesuses were not so doable after all. I had a conundrum on my hands. I could power through it with clenched teeth and wishful thinking. I could hold on for dear life and hope I would make it through with some faith intact. Or . . . I didn't know what the other option was. Maybe there wasn't one.

Then I began to hear the gospel message afresh, and it was like I was breathing pure oxygen for the first time after years of slow spiritual asphyxiation. I began to hear bits of faithful preaching here and there. I devoured books that highlighted what Jesus had already done on behalf of sinners. I squared what I'd read with Scripture, and I began to breathe a little easier.

Still I was having a hard time getting the stink of muddled Christian messages out of my nostrils. The "yes-grace-but" type of messages that hold out the gift of salvation and forgiveness but in the next breath dole out Christian life checklists. This is like getting the perfect gift, only to have the giver of the gift harass you to pay them back.

Have you ever been away from your house and returned only to realize there's a stink in your own home? We become so accustomed to our surroundings that we often don't notice when our couch smells like a wet dog has been lounging around with his paws up on the coffee table while he was smoking cigars. "Yes-grace-but" messages have a way of stinking up the joint. Don't miss my point though. This is not a complaint about a pastor's public speaking skills. A faithful pastor can be a poor orator and still deliver a gospel-rich message that feeds God's people. If you get three square meals a day on a regular basis—something simple, like a little bit of protein, a starch, and some sides of green veggies—lo and behold, over time you will be nourished and you will grow.[8]

When it comes down to it, I'd rather get a poorly spoken sermon from a bumbling preacher preparing simple nourishing meals week after week than a savvy preacher serving horse-pill-sized spiritual vitamins on a silver platter that are just going to choke me anyway. I want someone who delivers Christ crucified and the forgiveness of sins. You can have your slick, well-spoken pastor delivering a Christian pep talk; I don't want the false buzz of week in and week out energy-drink preaching. If I needed a motivational talk, I'd listen to a Tony Robbins seminar. When I go to church, I need the message of death and resurrection over and over and over.

CONCLUSION

The Law can't produce what it demands. Sure, law lite can squeeze out some results for a while. Good sense and spiritual advice puts a Band-Aid on the problem. But as we've mentioned, it ends in pride or despair. The Law has to close all the back door efforts of earning, make you dead in your inability to be a Law-abiding Christian, and straight-up kill you. Dead. As severe as that is, the good news—the really good news!—is that the Law is not the last word. The gospel is. Grace is free, undeserved, and always surprising. Death may come, but God is in the resurrection business!

The resurrection message is easy to get wrong though. Many have in their minds that salvation is a one-time event (I walked the aisle and prayed the prayer). From there on out, staying in the club means you'll have to pay your dues and perfectly obey, or at least prove how committed you are through your works. But death and resurrection in the life of the Christian isn't a one-time event. That is, we are saved in a moment in time. We are being saved in the present, and we will be saved in the future. It's an ongoing, everyday process. The fringe benefit of this news is that the Law can't condemn the Christian anymore. It will accuse you for sure. You can be certain it will give you a measuring stick for holy perfection. But it will point you to Christ again where real perfection is found. The Law can no longer condemn you. In Christ, you are free.

A few years ago when I was still at the Movement Leader church franchise nursing a bad case of spiritual burnout, I came across a lecture that pulled me out of the spiritual gag-reflex brought on by all the law and gospel confusion surrounding me. It was Rod Rosenbladt's "The Gospel for Those Broken by the Church."[9] This message was so refreshing to me that I've listened to it at least a dozen times. This message put the feeling of a law-gospel confused Christianity into perspective for me in a way that I can only characterize as paradigm shifting. Up until that point, I'd done a good bit of self-study on the subject, but Rosenbladt's presentation codified the whole subject almost perfectly. In the last third of the recording, he perfectly sums up when and how the gospel must be delivered to law-crushed believers. Rosenbladt says, "CFW Walther said that as soon as the law has done its crushing work, the gospel is to be instantly preached or said to such a man or woman—instantly! Walther said that in the very moment that the pastor senses that the law has done its killing work, he is to placard Christ and his cross and blood to the trembling, the despairing, the broken."[10] Then Rosenbladt gives the following long string of gospel-rich passages that put a lump in my throat every time:

- "Take heart, my son; your sins are forgiven" (Matthew 9:2).
- "The Son of Man came not to be served but to serve, and to give his life as a ransom for many" (Matthew 20:28).
- "Fear not, little flock, for it is your Father's good pleasure to give you the kingdom" (Luke 12:32).
- "Come to me, all who labor and are heavy laden, and I will give you rest" (Matthew 11:28).
- "a bruised reed he will not break, and a smoldering wick he will not quench" (Matthew 12:20).
- "'...remember me when you come into your kingdom.' And he said to him, 'Truly, I say to you,

today you will be with me in paradise'" (Luke 23:42–43).

- "It is finished" (John 19:30).
- "Christ redeemed us from the curse of the law by becoming a curse for us" (Galatians 3:13).
- "He himself bore our sins in his body on the tree . . ." (1 Peter 2:24).
- "For our sake he made him to be sin who knew no sin . . ." (2 Corinthians 5:21).
- "So in Christ Jesus you are all children of God, through faith. For as many of you as were baptized into Christ have put on Christ" (Galatians 3:26–27).
- "For by grace you have been saved through faith. And this is not your own doing; it is the gift of God, not a result of works, so that no one may boast" (Ephesians 2:8–9).
- "And to the one who does not work but believes in him who justifies the ungodly, his faith is counted as righteousness" (Romans 4:5).
- "For we hold that one is justified by faith apart from works of the law" (Romans 3:28).
- "yet we know that a person is not justified by works of the law but through faith in Jesus Christ" (Galatians 2:16).
- "But now the righteousness of God has been manifested apart from the law . . . the righteousness of God through faith in Jesus Christ for all who believe" (Romans 3:21–22).
- "Therefore, since we have been justified by faith, we have peace with God through our Lord Jesus Christ" (Romans 5:1).
- "There is therefore now no condemnation for those who are in Christ Jesus" (Romans 8:1).

OK. Deep breath. Doesn't that feel better?

To be put to death and resurrected in Christ means there's no need for pretension. The older I get, the more I realize how little I actually know and how much I have to learn. Of course the Christian life isn't all about learning, intellectualizing, or cracking a spiritual code. We're not simply disembodied brains on a stick; we're whole people—mind, body, and spirit. It's not as if God only puts out the welcome mat of heaven for those with "correct theology." To believe that is—ahem—pride. No, the point of deep theological truths is to connect us to Jesus. The real flesh and blood who died and rose for you and me, Jesus.

So until we hit the big dirt-nap jackpot and meet him face-to-face, we can know that he has sent the Spirit—the Spirit who comforts us with Scriptures that testify to Jesus's work for us. The same Spirit that sends the words of a faithful preacher sailing into our ears to comfort broken hearts. The Spirit who nourishes us with bread and wine, and cleanses us in baptism. That's all pretty simple stuff. And it rarely feels like emotional or spiritual fireworks. But the more I'm able to grasp God's presence in and through these simple means by faith, the more confident I am that he's feeding me spiritually. He's drawing me to himself—bloody gauze and all—and holding me close. Even when life is backward, upside down, broken to bits, and depressing as hell, he's not done with you and me. And that is a great comfort.

The simplicity of the means by which the Spirit is at work (through the Word, water, bread, and wine) has broken open my pride because they're truth delivering means that have nothing whatsoever to do with my brain power or ability to theologize myself out of the darkness. What was once pride now makes way for humility. And if not humility, at least the process of being humbled.

Sometimes all we can say in the mess of it all is, "Lord, to whom shall we go? You have the words of eternal life, and we have believed, and have come to know, that you are the Holy One of God" (John 6:68–69). And in that confession, even when we're not fully able to understand, the claustropho-bic despair that takes the air out of the room breaks up. The despair is replaced with an expansive, fresh air of hope . . . true hope, not the false, conditional, asphyxiating promises of all the imposter Jesuses.

Chapter 8
Humility and Hope

I wrote this book in large part because I need this reminder myself not to go back to the yolk of slavery that Paul talks about. "For freedom Christ has set us free; stand firm therefore, and do not submit again to a yoke of slavery" (Galatians 5:1). The gospel message is true whether you believe it day in and day out or not. I hope and pray you avail yourself to the lavish love of God. It is yours in Christ for free, for real, forever.

THE PAIN AND BEAUTY OF THE GIFT OF HUMILITY

As a teenager, I came to Life Coach Jesus to get an attaboy for living the right kind of life. It took many years to realize that the real Jesus was inviting me to be a part of a bigger story than the story of me. I came to Checklist Jesus hoping to complete that "one thing" so I could prove to myself and others that I was truly a committed disciple of Jesus. It turned out the checklist was crushing and demoralizing. I came to Visionary Jesus and Movement Leader Jesus to secure a sense of belonging within an exciting movement of God, but leaders fail, and institutions crumble. Each picture of the spiritual life promised more than it could deliver. I thought life would end up more fulfilling spirituality. Ultimately, chasing after the false Jesuses left me prideful, despairing, or ping-ponging between the two, depending on whether I was having a bad day or not. I can cover up the disappointment of getting sold a bill of goods with sarcasm (hence, the book subtitle), but it pains me to look back over a couple decades of my life of faith. In these two-plus decades, I've lived through the death of each false savior. The process has been slow, painful, disorienting, and sometimes crushing. Reflecting back, I see a common theme: I'm hardwired toward autonomy and pride. I wonder if you can relate?

I won't dare claim humility for myself—that would only prove the opposite. But I do have faith that as my prideful expectations of God are put to death, I'm humbled. And the path I've been on has been littered with a fair share of little deaths. As these little deaths pile up, I've been taught by Jesus in the school of faith that God is kneading something good into me, like yeast into a lump of dough.

Whether that counts as humility, I don't know. I'll let God be the judge of that. All I can say is that though the disappointment as expectations are put to death is truly painful, it's ultimately freeing. I expected a life of faith would feel more fulfilling, include more successes, consolations, and high fives. That somehow it'd feel like . . . like progress. But as I go through the little deaths of life, God resurrects me. As my pride is squashed, it's slowly being replaced with a sense of humor, humility, and dependence on my faithful Savior who truly has paid it all and done it all.

The same is true for you: you've gone through and will go through little deaths. But from death, God resurrects you. As pride is squashed, humility, humor, and dependence on another (that's faith, right?) blossom forth. Our false Jesuses drive us to pride or despair. God comes along and grows us up a little bit, and it hurts. Like growing pains. Like falling down, eating the pavement and learning to take a deep breath, shake it off, and live with the scabs like a big kid. God allows us to face some bumps and bruises in life. Death even. The little "d" deaths—the loss of a job, health, or relationships—and the big "D" death that inevitably comes to claim us all. He humbles us. Even in this very moment as I'm fighting this humbling process, I'm comforted to know I'm not the only clown in town. I hope you're comforted too.

As I think about what it means to know Jesus and follow him, I'm reminded of Jesus's parable of the tax collector and the Pharisee at the altar. The one guy can't even bring himself to lift his head and asks for mercy. The Pharisee thanks God he's not like the other guy. I'm not sure I have a friend, relative, or neighbor that I compare myself to in the way the Pharisee compares himself to his lowlife altar-call mate. Instead, it's more like "Imagination-Me" gets pitted against "Reality-Me." "What? That guy? I'm not that guy. I'm the good guy." Ah, well, God's still working on me. Things are still hazy, but I think I'm beginning to see and have faith he's not done with me yet. He's not done with you either, my friend.

Let's read the passage and see what we can learn about the nature of humility. And maybe on an ever deeper level, death and resurrection.

> "Two men went up into the temple to pray, one a Pharisee and the other a tax collector. The Pharisee, standing by himself, prayed thus: 'God, I thank you that I am not like other men, extortioners, unjust, adulterers, or even like this tax collector. I fast twice a week; I give tithes of all that I get.' But the tax collector, standing far off, would not even lift up his eyes to heaven, but beat his breast, saying, 'God, be merciful to me, a sinner!' I tell you, this man went down to his house justified, rather than the other. For everyone who exalts himself will be humbled, but the one who humbles himself will be exalted." (Luke 18:10–14)

The big idea of this parable seems to be the virtue of humility.[1] You've probably heard sermons on this passage. Sermons that say "Don't think too highly of yourself like the Pharisee, you're saved by Jesus, not your goodness. So be humble like the other guy. What God wants from you is a little bit of humility."

Humility, yes, but maybe the deeper point of this parable is death and resurrection.[2] Both the Pharisee and the tax collector are dead meat. The difference is that the bad guy in the story knows it while the religious guy (or "good" guy) does not. All the tax collector did was say, "I'm a royal screw-up, God. Please forgive me." That's it. In theory, most of us like the idea that anyone can come to God and be forgiven. Let's think about it in a contemporary context.

THE TAX COLLECTOR IN CONTEMPORARY TERMS

Consider what the tax collector was all about. These guys were social turds. Often the tax man was from among the Jewish people, but he worked for the Romans. Basically, he was considered a traitor. They charged above and beyond the tax, gave Caesar what was due him, and pocketed the rest. There is a fancy word for this—extortion.

Let's put it in contemporary perspective. Let's say you saw a guy going up to the altar after church for prayer. You recognized him because he was in the local news caught up in some kind of scandal related to organized crime. The cops could never quite pin him down, but everybody knew he was up to no good. Money laundering, black market dealings, and probably drug trafficking. If you saw him in church, you'd be shocked, at the least. If you're a kind soul, maybe your heart would go out to him because after all, he's a sinner in need of grace just like anybody else. I wonder how much charity we'd give this guy in real life though.[3] I mean, theoretically we love the idea of grace for bad guys, but in reality, I wonder how tough it would be to look the guy in the eye, shake his hand, and give him a smile.

THE PHARISEE AS UPSTANDING CHURCHGOER

Now let's take a crack at the Pharisees. The poor Pharisees. Those guys always get such a bad rap. They've been so caricatured we're often unable to identify with them ourselves.

What if, instead of erecting a cardboard cutout version of a jerk-faced, uptight religious person with their undies riding too high, we replace upstanding, educated Christian pastor in its place (or ourselves at our trying-hardest-to-be-good best).

Think about it. The world would be a lot better off with more of these kinds of people. They tend to be good citizens in the community. They mow their grass regularly, give to the church, preach faithfully Sunday after Sunday, and have well-adjusted kids.[4] Sure, maybe they're a little bit square, but these guys help make our communities better. However, there are a couple problems with this guy. He doesn't understand that he's a dead duck just like Organized Crime guy. And because others see him as a community asset rather than a liability, no one would ever guess God might actually have a beef with him.

THE FORFEIT OF SELF-JUSTIFICATION

God isn't impressed with the Pharisee's spiritual and civic moral duties report card. And do you know why? Because God does not grade on some kind of curve. Instead, he gives an impossible demand (as we discovered two chapters ago). You either get an A or an F.[5] There's no in-between. Organized Crime Guy already knows he's flunked. He already knows he's seen as a scab of society. He gets sneers from the old ladies in the checkout line at the grocery store. He's keenly aware that if the Feds ever caught up to his shenanigans, he'd rot in prison, and whatever punishment he had coming to him, he'd deserve. And yet, he gets to go home forgiven and justified. No matter how many times he comes up to the altar and goes through the routine.

Meanwhile, the Upright Citizen Pastor—as nice of a guy as he is—is self-justifying. But forgiveness and reconciliation with God only go one way, no matter what one's moral or spiritual condition. Organized Crime Guy brought all the right things to the table: his sin and his need for forgiveness. Upright Citizen Pastor came with too much baggage: a little bit of sin (a few mistakes here and there that he's working on) and a good report card. This will never work. God gets us right with himself and brings us into the kingdom all on his own. No behaviors on our part—whether it's habitual carousing or orphan adopting—can secure our heavenly citizenship.

Trying to improve a moral quality is altogether different than giving up, dying, and experiencing death, which is the opposite of trying. Dying is a passive enterprise on our part that God can work with and from. There's a resurrection on the other side of our death. But for the Pharisee to feel self-assured by the consistency with which he's taken his spiritual vitamins (and how he's getting "better") shows that he doesn't understand how God justifies someone. The tax collector may never take a spiritual vitamin in his life, yet, he knows in himself he has no moral ground to stand on for acceptance with God. He knows he's "dead in sin" and calls out in a last-ditch effort for God to have mercy. And yet he's the one that goes home justified. I don't know about you, but that sounds both scandalous and too good to be true. I'm beginning to believe more and more that it *is* true.

God's Kindness in Frustrating Our Plans

Over these decades, God has been kind to put my false Jesuses to death and frustrate my expectations. He's caused me to step into the experience of the scumbag tax collector. What I'm discovering is the grotesque truth that too often I love the gifts of God more than I love God himself. I'm more caught up in the gift itself than in the Giver of the gift. I wince with every keystroke of that sentence—it seems like a lightning bolt should obliterate me at any moment. All I can really say is "God, be merciful to me, a sinner!" I remember God's patience; he's not done with me yet. I remember the apostle Peter—a guy who couldn't curb his diarrhea of the mouth to save his life. The guy who up and denied Jesus three times. I think of doubting Thomas, who would not believe Jesus had been raised from the dead until he could put a finger into the wound in Jesus's side. If Jesus had patience with those jokers, if he really loved them, maybe he'll love me too. And he does. I know in my mind—according to a correct view of God that he loves me, and yet, sometimes I struggle to believe. Lord, I believe. Help my unbelief (Mark 9:24).

So, pride? I've got me some. I'd rather not admit that, but it's true. It's safer to reflect back on my past mistakes and all the things I've learned along the way. Yeah, I was a chump and bought into the lies of the culture and of my own heart. I thought God was signed up to my life story. Turns out he has different plans. My pride runs deep, and God is digging at my roots right now, present tense. And I suppose I ought to go first. Maybe you can fill in the blanks with your own story.

PRESENT TENSE PRIDE

One surefire reason I know I'm prideful is that I've recently begun to come to terms with the fact that I'm virtually unable to receive any sort of criticism from my wife. Either real or perceived, I have no backbone for it, and she pays for it with my cold silence. For those taking notes, this is not a recipe for marital bliss.

In my twenties, I thought I was quite a catch. A sort of Lloyd Dobler,[6] sensitive, arty type. My future wife was going to be blessed to have me as her guy! I'm not so sure my real-life wife would agree. We love each other, and we're committed. Our backstory has taken fifteen years to build, and it's complex. But life together is not fun right now. I'm waking up to the fact that it hasn't been fun for a long, long time.

As I face the clichés of middle age (I hate being a cliché), I find myself disappointed. Life is not as I thought it would turn out. I thought I'd be happier and more fulfilled. As these intense pressures of life loom heavy, it's squeezed my pride to the top. "Sure," I say to myself, "I may not be perfect, but at least I'm not *that* guy—the cold, distant husband . . ." But then reality sets in, "Uh, oops. Actually, I am that guy." My self-justifying activity abounds. I'm acting like Upright Citizen Pastor. I'm acting like Good Husband guy. The cold reality is that I'm the tax collector. I'm the Organized Crime Guy. And that means I'm actually the Cold, Emotionally Distant Husband guy. I don't like owning up to this reality, but it's all I've got to bring to the altar. I clamor for dear life to send the signal to myself and to the world that I may not be perfect, but I'm not like *him*. I really don't want to believe I do this. But I do. It's ugly. And yet, I think I might be getting better. Maybe brokenness is kneading a little bit of humility into me yet.

When I see the ugliness in my life, I can call it like it is and die to it because I know that my Savior isn't going to turn me away. I can run to him and grieve my sin and sins committed against me. I can grieve the losses and the disappointments of life, knowing he hears them all. He doesn't roll his eyes at my plight (or yours) or tap his foot in frustration waiting for me to get my act together. He'll love and welcome you and me just as we are. And we'll go home justified just like that tax crook. I have hope. You and I both have hope. Because you and I have a Savior big enough to deal with our death(s). He is the resurrection. He is the life. And now our life is bound to him and to his life-giving Spirit.

So let's be content to give up the game. To quit self-justifying. It hurts, I know. I've got a death grip on my perceived self. But you and I, we've got nothing to give back to God when it comes to holiness. It's OK. None of us do. We're loved anyway. Our holiness is not achieved but received. And this is our hope: the love of God in Jesus Christ for you and for me despite where we are on our journey.

Hope Where There Was None

Therefore, since we have been justified by faith, we have peace with God through our Lord Jesus Christ. Through him we have also obtained access by faith into this grace in which we stand, and we rejoice in hope of the glory of God. Not only that, we rejoice in our sufferings, knowing that suffering produces endurance, and endurance produces character, and character produces hope, and hope does not put us to shame, because God's love has been poured into our hearts through the Holy Spirit who has been given to us. (Romans 5:1–5)

OK, here's a little more honesty for you. I've been avoiding this last portion on hope like a scruffy mutt avoids a bath. Why? Because I don't feel like I have anything to offer right now. Finding sustenance in life feels a little bit like picking through a garbage heap right now. It's feeling a little more like an embarrassing fall down a flight of stairs in slow motion than a fist-pumping-the-sky climb to personal victory.

Here's some background. At the time of this writing, I'm unemployed for the second time in the last couple years. I've had to scrounge bits of part-time work for a year. My wife has had baffling health problems associated with extreme fatigue, chronic pain, and vertigo. There's a significant rift with extended family over a decade-long conflict. Our marriage is not so hot (I've been given permission to say this). I'm finally beginning to understand just a little bit what it's like to be married to me. I'll give you a hint: I'm a grump, I'm distant, and I'm emotionally closed off (as I mentioned previously). Not the recipe for fanning the flame of romance. Now try that on for fifteen years. Thankfully, we attend a church full of warm, compassionate people who help us keep our sights on our Savior. We have wise, loving friends with big, empathy-filled hearts. We're doing hard, necessary work with professional counselors.

The cherry on top of this steaming pile of doo-doo involves having to quietly leave a megachurch we were a part of for seventeen years. Well, we either left quietly or were pushed out, depending on how you look at it, I guess. Over the course of the following year the same church imploded as years of domineering, toxic leadership among some of the executive pastors finally caught up with them. We watched the ship going down, and it was traumatizing. Many of us had lived in anticipation that the corruption and domineering in the church's leadership was going to get better. Certain leaders assured us that there were big, happy surprises ahead. I was told a very important meeting was upcoming where ongoing issues and concerns would be addressed. We'd held out hope that the downward spiral would self-correct somehow. It was exciting to anticipate that maybe we'd get our church back. It was like Santa coming to town.

But Santa never came with presents. Instead, Santa burnt the house down. Instead of goodies, he left a flaming brown paper bag on the front porch full of dog crap.[7] Merry Christmas, church! Like I told friends recently, we'll probably walk with a limp for the rest of our lives after that one. This is the stuff that therapy sessions are made for! And when I take an honest assessment of the last twenty years, I think it's safe to say I've been legitimately depressed during that time. Not the I-can't-get-out-of-bed type of depression or I-feel-like-I'm-going-to-die panic attack depression, but a low, steady, dull grind that I've lugged around for decades. Everything's not awesome.[8]

I am not telling you this to garner sympathy, but out of a desire to be completely honest and transparent about the realities of my present tense life. If I'm honest, maybe it will free you to be honest about your life too. Because the relational train crash, the church-sabotaging narcissists, and the job pink slip may come your way too. That's real life in the real world. When we get honest about these kinds of things maybe we can get free and see true hope instead of grasping at false hopes that ultimately let us down.

As I've already said, I've made some surprising discoveries as I've written this book. I told my editor recently that I likened this project to a simple trip. I'd mapped out a little getaway from Seattle to California. Instead, I wound up taking a transatlantic flight across the globe, missed several flights, and had some all-night layovers in obscure airports reeking of equal parts unwashed armpits and cheap cologne and having to sleep on 1980s carpeting littered with flattened chewing gum and flickering overhead florescent lighting to find my way. In hindsight, I don't think there was any other way to make the journey. I began thinking about this project as a snarky theological corrective to a problem that I've seen within Christian culture. I imagined unbridled magic coming from my fingertips. Then I'd turn in my manuscript in glory and clink glasses with my friends over my intellectual achievement.

What I discovered is that I'm the clueless chump that I set out to correct in the first place. I bought into the lies of our culture, my own spiritually two-timing heart, and shallow Christianity. Now I'm disappointed. I feel duped. Some days I feel angry enough to break large panes of glass for a little bit of relief (though I haven't indulged . . . yet). I guess the shorthand for the hodgepodge of emotions that I'm having is midlife crisis. Welcome to the crisis party.

This section is supposed to be about hope. Yet, I don't feel any hope. If there's any hope, it exists out there somewhere, but not here under my rib cage. My failing heart isn't factory specified to generate hope on its own. I have a passive ability for hope, kind of like a pot of water has the capacity to boil once the stove is turned on.[9] But I'm beginning to see that maybe this isn't such a bad thing. Because my hope is transferring from temporal things to things eternal.

So writing about hope is going to require what feels like some heavy lifting. If you'll forgive me, I'm going to lean on a couple of quotes for this one. In reference to the story of Jesus and the paralytic in Mark 2:1–12, an old friend used to say that when we're paralyzed by life, sometimes we need friends who will tear open a hole in the roof and lower us down in front of Jesus. We may not have the ability in ourselves to get in front of Jesus, but our friends can help us get to him.[10] So, I'd like to lean on some friends for this one, if you don't mind. (I don't personally know these people, but they've written to my experience in a way that makes them feel like friends to me).

I suppose not everything is devoid of hope. There's a special moment each week I can't take for granted. It's when I stand at the front of the church with a morsel of torn bread doused in cheap red wine at the altar. The communion servers awkwardly try to maintain eye contact as they tell me, "Christ's body, for you . . . Christ's blood shed for you." Then I dunk that bit of bread really well so that the wine drips onto my hand. It reminds me of the blood of my Savior who bled and died one day long ago up on a lonely hill between two criminals for me and for you. I'm so spiritually inept that I need the tangible reminder of that simple moment. I need to know that my Savior bleeding and dying for me was just as real as that piece of wine-drenched bread in my hand. And in some mysterious way, beyond human logic, in that moment I am spiritually fed by the body and blood of Jesus Christ. I cling for dear life to the truth that my redemption is as sure as Jesus's resurrection.[11]

On some Sundays, unfortunately, I just go through the motions. I wait my turn as the congregation takes turns filing up by row. I take a bit of bread, dip it into the wine cup, pop it in my mouth, and go back to my pew. It's a routine. On other Sundays, it takes everything in me not to burst into tears. Taking communion each week is my hope; it's a fleeting moment colliding with eternal truth. That a poor, homeless Jewish man two thousand years ago came to put everything right with the world. He was horribly mistreated, condemned, and unjustly executed. And yet, this man Jesus, he is God incarnate. And he lived and died and was raised for the sake of his love and resurrection for the world, for you, for me. And as he died, we must die. But like him, we will rise again (Romans 6:23). This is hope.

The Hope of a Story Bigger Than My Own

Upon my teenaged conversion, I'd hoped that Life Coach Jesus would give me an owner's manual. Principles to live a successful, fulfilled life. Now I know I can't hope for every answer I may want for my life story. But I have hope in a Savior who says I'm a part of a story bigger than the one I've tried to write for myself. My life story is ultimately not about me, but about him,[12] and he has a way better story to tell than I do.

One of the most deeply enriching things for my faith over the past few years was being a part of a ministry created by my good friend, Mike Wilkerson, called Redemption Groups.[13] The guiding biblical theme throughout these groups is the Exodus. In the story of the Exodus, God's people languished under Egyptian slavery for four hundred years. They lived in brutal conditions and were forced into backbreaking labor. (Imagine living in a culture where all your people have ever known is slavery. As a white American living in the twenty-first century with the heat on and a pantry full of food, it's unfathomable.) Ultimately, after God sent a series of dramatic plagues, Pharaoh relented and let the people go. But Pharaoh changed his mind (once again) and chased after the people. He hems them in at the Red Sea. There God displays his grand finale, the parting of the Red Sea. The people cross over on dry ground while Pharaoh's army is destroyed in the ensuing collapse of the walls of water. God's people are free! Then the realities of desert life set in. Getting out of Egypt was a pretty great miracle to behold. But now they're in the desert. This was not the Promised Land they had hoped for.

In some ways we're like the Israelites, aren't we? We can bag on the Israelites as faithless dolts, but I'm sure that if put in the same situation I would be as control-freakish as they were. If I were told to "just trust God to provide," and not have any food in the fridge for the next day, I'd be anxious. Heck, I get anxious when there is food in the fridge and the bank account starts getting low! And yet, God remains faithful to the people. He provides for them day by day, and ultimately, he brings them to the Promised Land. It takes forty years, but he does it.

Along the way God shared himself with them and pointed to his great provision in Jesus—the shed blood of the lamb that averted death, the manna from heaven, the water from the rock. All were tangible signs to God's people of God's presence among them and the salvation to come. Today, we see clearly what the Israelites only glimpsed: Jesus is the Lamb of God who takes away the sins of the world. Jesus is the bread from heaven that satisfies forever. Jesus is the water of life—the spring that never runs dry.

How quickly I forget that Jesus is here with me now. Actually, I'm a lot more like the Israelites than I'd like to admit. I'd much prefer the guarantee of a regular paycheck and a full pantry. For now, it's "give us this day our daily bread," and God sends manna and quail. The hope that I have in this moment is not in my abilities to write my own story. My life-story-writing is abysmal right now. But God has written a story, and he's invited me into it. I may not always like the part that he has for me to play, but I have hope that just like the Exodus, God isn't through with his people yet. And I have hope, that even when I don't "feel" it, God's promised presence is with me. He is holding onto me, even when I lose my grip on him. He will not let me go.

There's a promised land up ahead flowing with milk and honey. By extension, he isn't done with me yet. He is an intervening God. He is a loving, providing God. Like the Israelites, I'm in a desert. It's a first-world problems kind of desert for sure, but a desert nonetheless with a Promised Land to come. I've got to keep my eye on the prize that is the Promised Land—the perfection of God's people and the renewal of all creation,[14] which has already been inaugurated in Jesus. I'm holding onto that hope for dear life right now.

Hope in the One Who Lived and Died—for Me

Have you ever felt as though God is disappointed in you? I have. But maybe you and I are looking at things all wrong. Years ago a preacher said something that made a lot of sense out of my wrongheaded view of God's disappointment with me.[15] Here's the picture: Have you ever seen a parent's irrational joy as they celebrate their child's first steps? How bizarre would it be if, instead of celebrating, the two parents scold their toddler for getting it all wrong. "Keep your balance, Timmy! No, no! Not like that! Center your weight! You never listen to me! Why don't you ever listen!?" This would be one bizarre sight. No, when a child takes their first steps, the parents act like their kid invented a cure for cancer. And they share with the whole world through their Facebook feed that their kid is a pint-sized superhero. Isn't this a closer picture of the heart of God? Once we belong to Jesus, he doesn't look through the lenses of our own perfection, but through the perfection of Jesus. When we step, step, step and fall, we can get back up again knowing our proud, beaming father is broadcasting to the world that we're "walking."[16]

Elyse Fitzpatrick put it well in her book *Because He Loves Me*, a favorite in the Johnson household. I'll quote at length because it's that good.

> I'll admit that sometimes I cast about for assurance when I feel the creeping doubt and despair that infect my heart as I struggle with sin. When I look through all the closets of my soul and all I find is lovelessness, I know that I don't have any claim to God's love on my own. The only truth that can assuage is this: I know that God loves his Son. Even though there are times when I wonder how God can love me, I know that he loves his Son, and because he has made a formal, legal declaration that I'm in him, then I must continue to tell myself and believe that he loves me because of him. My only other option is to say that he doesn't

love his Son at all. But the truth is that the pronounce-
ment he made over him, "This is my beloved Son, with
whom I am well pleased" (Matt. 3:17), he has now
made over us: "This is my beloved daughter, this is my
beloved son, all in whom I am well pleased." Will God
ever push us away or keep us at arm's length? Would
he push his Son away? Will God ever fail to hear our
prayer? Does he hear his Son's? Is he disgusted with us
and disappointed that he ever adopted us? Does Jesus
disgust and disappoint him?[17]

Well said, sister. To answer the question she poses at the end
of the quote: No, God is not disgusted with Jesus. According
to this lovely logic, by extension, he's not disgusted with us for
step-step-step biffing it. I sure hope she's right about Jesus's
acceptance before the Father transferring to me. I'm banking
my whole life on the belief that God is pleased with me, as
messed up as I am, on account of Jesus who lived perfectly in
my place.

CONCLUSION

Well into my twenties I put a false hope in association with a
"movement." It carved out a sense of belonging and identity
for me. But my hope is not in belonging to a fleeting moment
within a movement, but to my Savior who is eternally at work,
by his Spirit, despite outward appearances. Throughout this
book, we've considered the reality that God is often at work
in counterintuitive ways. We often chase after big shiny things
or "important" people who make us feel good about ourselves
and guarantee us a table with the cool kids. But all across
Scripture, God is working in and through weakness. He is
working in and through the deadbeats, the moral reprobates,
and the homeless guys. Who woulda thunk it?

The apostle Paul says in 1 Corinthians that the cross of Jesus is foolishness (1:18) and the weakness of God is stronger than men (1:25). A few verses later Paul says,

> But God chose what is foolish in the world to shame the wise; God chose what is weak in the world to shame the strong; God chose what is low and despised in the world, even things that are not, to bring to nothing things that are, so that no human being might boast in the presence of God. And because of him you are in Christ Jesus, who became to us wisdom from God, righteousness and sanctification and redemption, so that, as it is written, "Let the one who boasts, boast in the Lord." (1 Corinthians 1:27–31)

We look for proof of where God is at work, don't we? We see power, influence, and git-'er-done attitude in an expertly tailored Italian business suit and say, "That's where God is at work!" And yet, God keeps showing up in weak and despised things. As Martin Luther writes, "The cross is not simply the end of the journey in our quest for righteousness—not simply the destination of a happy outcome of life with God for us dead sinners; it is also the means by which the journey is made, and the experience of the journey itself."[18]

The Christian life is cross shaped. It's going to be a bit of a grind, and we can't always trust our senses to reveal where God has "shown up." Often he reveals himself where we least expect it. Where has God shown his glory most clearly? Two thousand years ago when a baby was born in a barn. Imagine the smell. Was there an ancient equivalent of hand-sanitizer? And yet, there's a baby lying there in hay. If that weren't scandalous enough, the glory is best displayed at the cross of Jesus Christ. The equivalent of the modern-day electric chair. From the outside looking in, barnyard births and executions are not where you find winning résumé-building moments. Yet, as Carl Trueman has put it, "If the cross of Christ, the most evil

act in human history, can be in line with God's will and be the
source of the decisive defeat of the very evil that caused it, then
any other evil can also be subverted to the cause of good."[19]
God is at work despite the pee-drenched straw, the stubbed
toes, and the waiting in funeral parlors. When your life is in
the crapper, when your church is torn apart by wolves, God
is present even if you can't see it or feel his presence. I have
hope in the trials of life that he still makes beauty out of ashes
(Isaiah 61:3).

In the past I have put hope in leaders with a successful, stra-
tegic vision—a vision of a future church, but not the church as it
existed in reality. Their vision destroyed a church loved by many.
A church built on the backs of good people who were used, dis-
carded, and then blamed for the failure. Thank God none of
us has to hope in a fleeting vision. Instead, we can hope in the
secure reality that God has and is reconciling all things to himself in Jesus. This story line is secure. Jesus himself said, "Take
heart; I have overcome the world" (John 16:33) and "All authority on heaven and earth has been given to me" (Matthew 28:18).

We are living in the reality of an already/not-yet kingdom.
Or put in fancy-schmancy theological terms, we exist within
the tension called "inaugurated eschatology."[20] This means that
Jesus has already established his kingdom and the new creation
has begun, but it's not a done deal yet. Imagine a state of the art,
heat-seeking missile launcher. Once the computer locks into
a target and launches that missile, it will find its target. High-
tech weaponry may not be the best analogy, but you get the
picture. Our lives in the present exist before the missile gets to
the target. But it's a guarantee that it will get there.

In the meantime, we still lug around decrepit bodies
plagued by gout and indigestion, churches get ruined by megalomania, and Thanksgiving with the family this year is going
to be as awkward as it always is when Uncle Mort drinks too
much wine and starts airing family grievances again. Still, God
has a way of becoming present even in the rough edges of life.
As the genius poet/singer-songwriter Leonard Cohen has said

in his song "Anthem": "There is a crack, a crack in everything, that's how the light gets in."

Like the Israelites in the wilderness, God has set his people free. Now the trick is to live a life of freedom amidst the brokenness within ourselves and the world around us. Things get a little weird, painful, and confusing. God's not done. He's got this. And he's got you and me. We don't need someone's vision for the future of the church. It's already defined. Now all we do is keep telling the story.

So underneath the crusty layers of this midlife crisis, there is a little bit of hope buried after all. With any luck, maybe this little crisis party of mine is on the verge of a big win: the dream job, the blissful marriage, the loving church community, and the caring family. Whatever the outcomes, I still have a place in this world in Jesus Christ as a loved, forgiven, and adopted son. And so do you. All we have to do is give him our nothing—even our death—and he answers it with resurrection.

I've had the wrong picture of Christianity for a long time. It's quite possible I still do. It feels like a lot of wasted time, but I know God can whip things into shape in that all-things-work-together way of his (Romans 8:28). Whatever the case—and I know it sounds cliché—I can give it all to Jesus and know that somehow it's going to work out. Our deceased friend Robert Capon gives us one last beautiful quote,

> Trust him. And when you have done that, you are living the life of grace. No matter what happens to you in the course of that trusting—no matter how many waverings you may have, no matter how many suspicions that you have bought a poke with no pig in it, no matter how much heaviness and sadness your lapses, vices, indispositions, and bratty whining may cause you—you believe simply that Somebody Else, by his death and resurrection, has made it all right, and you just say thank you and shut up. The whole slop-closet full of mildewed performances (which is

all you have to offer) is simply your death; it is Jesus who is your life. If he refused to condemn you because your works were rotten, he certainly isn't going to flunk you because your faith isn't so hot. You can fail utterly, therefore, and still live the life of grace. You can fold up spiritually, morally, or intellectually and still be safe. Because at the very worst, all you can be is dead—and for him who is the Resurrection and the Life, that just makes you his cup of tea.[21]

Now it's your turn. Maybe, like me, you're feeling ripped off by a false image of the Christian life. Maybe you're just beginning to come to terms with the fact that you've been sold an imitation Jesus. You've biffed it morally. Your faith and trust is teetering on a ledge. Thankfully, as much as it stings, God is merciful not to allow us to hold onto false saviors. But this is not a "fluffy clouds, bunnies, and butterflies" kind of mercy, but a severe mercy. It's a "rip the Band-Aid off a festering wound" kind of mercy. But I have to hope that once we catch our collective breaths a little bit, there's comfort and healing to come.

And may the peace of God that surpasses all understanding guard your hearts and minds in Christ Jesus (Philippians 4:7). Amen.

Endnotes

Preface

1. See Gerhard Forde's *On Being a Theologian of the Cross: Reflections on Luther's Heidelberg Disputation, 1518* (Grand Rapids, MI: Wm. B. Eerdmans Publishing Co., 1997).

The Problem

1. Matt Johnson, "Pastor of Disaster," *Christ Hold Fast.* http://www.christholdfast.org/blog/pastor-of-disaster.

2. John Calvin, *Institutes of the Christian Religion* I:XI.8, trans. Henry Beveridge (Peabody, MA: Hendrickson Publishing, 2008), 55.

3. Ethan Richardson, "Angels with an Incredible Capacity for Beer: A 1986 Interview with Brennan Manning," *Mockingbird*, May 19, 2016. http://www.mbird.com/2016/05/throwback-thursday-the-wittenburg-doors-1986-interview-with-brennan-manning/.

4. Thanks to Mike Wilkerson for this insight.

5. "The Heidelberg Disputation," *The Book of Concord: The Confessions of the Lutheran Church.* http://bookofconcord.org/heidelberg.php.

6. Oswald Bayer, "Justification: Basis and Boundary of Theology," in *By Faith Alone: Essays in Honor of Gerhard O. Forde*, eds. Joseph A. Burgess and Marc Kolden (Grand Rapids: Eerdmans, 2004), 72.

7. Adolphh Koeberle, *Quest for Holiness: A Biblical, Historical, and Systematic Investigation* (New York: Harper, 1936), 447.

8. L. D. Ross, Y. Lelkes, and A. G. Russell (2012): How Christians reconcile their personal political views and the teachings of their faith: Projection as a means of dissonance reduction. *Proceedings of the National Academy of Sciences* 109: 3616–22.

9. Scot McKnight, "The Jesus We'll Never Know," *Christianity Today*, April 9, 2010. http://www.christianitytoday.com/ct/2010/april/15.22.html?order=&start=1.

10. R. M. Schneiderman, "Flock Is Now a Fight Team in Some Ministries," *New York Times*, Feb. 1, 2010. http://www.nytimes.com/2010/02/02/us/02fight.html?_r=0.

11. Ibid.

12. Gerhard O. Forde, *On Being a Theologian of the Cross: Reflections on Luther's Heidelberg Disputation*, 1518 (Kindle Location 409). Kindle Edition.

13. Steven Paulson, *Luther for Armchair Theologians* (Louisville, KY: Westminster John Knox Press, 2004), 101.

14. Ibid., 102.

15. Robert Kolb, "Luther on the Theology of the Cross," *Lutheran Quarterly* 16:443.

16. Ibid.

17. Carl Trueman, "Luther's Theology of the Cross," *New Horizons*, October 2005. http://www.opc.org/new_horizons/NH05/10b.html.

18. Ibid.

19. Steven A. Hein, *The Christian Life: Cross or Glory?* (Irvine, CA: NRP Books, 2015), Kindle Location 122.

20. Paulson, *Luther for Armchair Theologians*, 101.

21. Ibid., 101.

22. Ibid., 102.

23. Rod Rosenbladt, "The Gospel for Those Broken by the Church," *1517, The Legacy Project*, Feb. 10, 2014.

https://www.1517legacy.com/rodrosenbladt/2014/02/
the-gospel-for-those-broken-by-the-church/.

Chapter 1

1. Christian Smith, Melinda Lundquist Denton, *Soul Searching: The Religious and Spiritual Lives of American Teenagers* (Oxford University Press, 2005), 162–63.

2. Elyse M. Fitzpatrick and Dennis E. Johnson, *Counsel from the Cross: Connecting Broken People to the Love of Christ* (Wheaton, IL: Crossway Books, 2009), 55.

3. This is a great saying from my old friend, James Noriega.

4. Joel Osteen, *Your Best Life Now* (New York: FaithWords, 2004), 10.

5. Rod Rosenbladt, "Law and Gospel in the Christian Life," *1517, The Legacy Project*. https://www.1517legacy. com/freebies/Rod%20Rosenbladt%20-%20Law%20and%20 Gospel%20in%20the%20Christian%20Life.mp3.

6. Contrary to (sometimes) popular belief, this statement is not found in the Bible, but was coined by Benjamin Franklin.

Chapter 2

1. Rick Paulas, "The Power Team Was the Bloody, Evangelical Freakshow That Ruled the 80s," *Vice*. http://www. vice.com/read/evangelical-freak-show-the-power-team-were-christian-superstars-of-the-80s-456.

Chapter 3

1. Barbara Ehrenreich calls this "irrational exuberance" in *Bright-Sided: How Positive Thinking Is Undermining America* (New York: Metropolitan Books, 2009), 50.

2. This idea comes from a quip in a church bulletin written by Pastor John Haralson.

3. Keep in mind that this is a quick, forty-thousand-foot glimpse of a fifteen-plus-year chunk of life. Tracing what went wrong at that church and why is not something easily explained. And the subject probably deserves its own book.

Chapter 4

1. Christian Conciliation expert Judy Dabler has rightly criticized the idea of flattery. Flattery doesn't cost the flatterer anything and puts the one who is being flattered in an awkward position. They are no longer a person, but someone who is "the very best at x, y, or z" who the flatterer benefits from. Flattery is impersonal, cheap, and doesn't require any sort of relationship.

2. Diane Langberg, "Narcissism and the Systems It Breeds," *Forum of Christian Leaders*. https://www.youtube.com/watch?v=4BU3pwBa0qU.

3. Dietrich Bonhoeffer, *Life Together* (New York: Harper & Row Publishers, 1954), 27.

4. Langberg, "Narcissism." https://soundcloud.com/kendall-beachey/narcissism-and-the-system-it.

Chapter 5

1. Jacques Ellul, *The Subversion of Christianity* (Grand Rapids, MI: Wm. B. Eerdmans Publishing Company, 1986), 69.

2. Thanks to Mike Wilkerson who was a great conversation partner throughout my book-writing process. Mike helped me develop this biblical theme of "worldliness" for this chapter.

3. The Lutheran Confession, *The Formula of Concord* defines election like this: "By the election of grace we mean this truth, that all those who by the grace of God alone, for Christ's sake, through the means of grace, are brought to faith, are justified, sanctified, and preserved in faith here in time, that all these have already from eternity been

endowed by God with faith, justification, sanctification, and preservation in faith, and this for the same reason, namely, by grace alone, for Christ's sake, and by way of the means of grace. That this is the doctrine of the Holy Scripture is evident from Eph. 1:3–7; 2 Thess. 2:13, 14; Acts 13:48; Rom. 8:28–30; 2 Tim. 1:9; Matt. 24:22–24 (cp. Form. of Conc. Triglot, p. 1065, Paragraphs 5, 8, 23; M., p. 705)."

4. Rod Rosenbladt, "Law and Gospel," *1517, The Legacy Project,* Feb. 10, 2014. https://www.1517legacy.com/rodrosenbladt/2014/02/law-and-gospel/.

5. Paulson, *Luther for Armchair Theologians,* 29.

Chapter 6

1. C. FitzSimons Allison, *Fear, Love and Worship,* 2nd ed. (Vancouver, BC: Regent College Publishing, 2003), 53.

2. Todd Wilken, *Issues, Etc. Journal* 5, No. 1.

3. Ibid., p .

4. For a good treatment of the "threefold uses of the law," see William Hordern, *Living By Grace* (Eugene, OR: Wipf and Stock Publishers, 2002), 112–23.

5. Gerhard O. Forde, *Where God Meets Man* (Minneapolis, MN: Augsburg Publishing House, 1972), 14.

6. Ibid., 14.

7. Ibid., 15.

8. William McDavid, Ethan Richardson, and David Zahl, *Law and Gospel: A Theology for Sinners and Saints* (Charlottesville, VA: Mockingbird Ministries, 2015), 18–19.

9. Paul F. M. Zahl, *A Short Systematic Theology* (Grand Rapids, MI: Wm. B. Eerdmans Publishing Company, 2000), 7.

10. Robert Farrar Capon, *Kingdom, Grace, Judgment: Paradox, Outrage, and Vindication in the Parables of Jesus* (Grand Rapids, MI: Wm. B. Eerdmans Publishing Company, 1988), 242.

11. Forde, *Where God Meets Man,* 9.

12. The giving of the Law, and the deep meaning to the original hearers, and the multifaceted nature of the Law is not something I aim to tackle. There are many scholarly works on this, and I'm in no way trying to give a definitive definition. For further reading on the subject, check out *Five Views on Law and Gospel* (Counterpoints: Bible and Theology), Gerhard O. Forde's *The Law-Gospel Debate: An Interpretation of Its Historical Development*, Thomas Schreiner's *40 Questions About Christians and Biblical Law* (40 Questions & Answers Series), and Werner Elert's *Law and Gospel*. What I'd like to do instead is consider what the Law does to people.

13. More often than not, I think this is a confusion. The Law is always good (as Paul says in Romans 7). We are the ones that are *not good*.

14. Paul F. M. Zahl, *Grace in Practice: A Theology of Everyday Life* (Grand Rapids, MI: Wm. B. Eerdmans Publishing Co., 2007), 16.

15. Capon, *Kingdom, Grace, Judgment*, 153.

Chapter 7

1. The opening of this chapter is adapted from my blog which can be found at http://therealmattjohnson.com/the-miracle-cure/.

2. C. F. W. Walther, *Law and Gospel: How to Read and Apply the Bible* (St. Louis, MO: Concordia Publishing House, 2009), 69.

3. Ibid., 49.

4. Corinthians 1:20.

5. Cohost Scott Keith recalled hearing this statement from his seminary professor, James Nestingen.

6. See Martin Luther's 1518 Heidelberg Disputation.

7. Heidelberg Disputation, thesis 26: http://bookofconcord.org/heidelberg.php#26.

8. I believe this idea comes from Robert Farrar Capon.

9. Rod Rosenbladt, "The Gospel for Those Broken by the Church," *1517, The Legacy Project*, Feb. 10, 2014. https://www.1517legacy.com/rodrosenbladt/2014/02/the-gospel-for-those-broken-by-the-church/.

10. Ibid.

Chapter 8

1. Capon, *Kingdom, Grace, Judgment* (Kindle Location 4355). Kindle Edition.

2. http://www.csec.org/index.php/archives/23-member-archives/700-robert-farrar-capon-program-3705.

3. Capon, *Kingdom, Grace, Judgment* (Kindle Locations 4379-4380). Kindle Edition.

4. Ibid.

5. This comes from a teaching series from Rod Rosenbladt given at Cathedral Church of the Advent in Birmingham, Alabama.

6. For those not in the know (or too young to understand the reference), Lloyd Dobler was a character played by John Cusak in Cameron Crowe's 1989 movie, *Say Anything*. Lloyd was basically a sensitive, yet intelligent, funny, complicated romantic teenager. Everybody liked him.

7. This imagery comes courtesy of Ryan Kearns.

8. "Everything's not awesome" is a play on a common theme in the *Lego Movie* in the song that says, "Everything Is Awesome!" The *Lego Movie*, directed by Phil Lord and Christopher Miller (2014), DVD.

9. Gerhard O. Forde, *On Being a Theologian of the Cross: Reflections on Luther's Heidelberg Disputation*, 1518 (Kindle Locations 660-661). Kindle Edition.

10. This comforting idea comes from my old friend and former colleague, James Noriega.

11. Mike Wilkerson, *Redemption: Freed by Jesus from the Idols We Worship and the Wounds We Carry* (Wheaton, IL: Crossway, 2011), 66.

12. Ibid., 26.

13. Redemption groups are intensive small groups that help people discover the love of God together amidst life's sin and suffering.

14. Wilkerson, *Redemption*, 37.

15. Matt Chandler, "Grace Driven Effort," *The Village Church*, June 6, 2010. http://thevillagechurch.net/resources/sermons/detail/grace-driven-effort/.

16. Ibid.

17. Elyse M. Fitzpatrick, *Because He Loves Me: How Christ Transforms Our Daily Life* (Wheaton, IL: Crossway Books, 2008), 73–74.

18. D. Martin Luthers Werke, *Kritische Getamtausgabe* (Weimarer Ausgabe) (Weimar: Hermann Böhlau Publishers, 1883–); Steven A. Hein, *The Christian Life: Cross or Glory?* (Irvine, CA: NRP Books, 2015), Kindle Location 122.

19. Carl R. Trueman, "Luther's Theology." http://www.opc.org/new_horizons/NH05/10b.html.

20. Wilkerson, *Redemption*, 37.

21. Robert Farrar Capon, *Between Noon and Three: Romance, Law, and the Outrage of Grace* (Grand Rapids, MI: Wm. B. Eerdmans Publishing Company, 1997), 291–92

Are you tired of
"do more, try harder" religion?

Key Life has only one message, to communicate the radical grace of God to sinners and sufferers. Because of what Jesus has done, God's not mad at you.

On radio, in print, on CDs and online, we're proclaiming the scandalous reality of Jesus' good news of radical grace...leading to radical freedom, infectious joy and surprising faithfulness to Christ.

For all things grace, visit us at **KeyLife.**